A. Daly

Cornell Studies in Classical Philology

EDITED BY

Frederick M. Ahl, Kevin Clinton, John E. Coleman,
Judith R. Ginsburg, G. M. Kirkwood, Gordon R. Messing,
Phillip Mitsis, Alan J. Nussbaum, Pietro Pucci,
Jeffrey S. Rusten, Winthrop Wetherbee

VOLUME XLIX

A Poetics of Transformation:
Prudentius and Classical Mythology
by Martha A. Malamud

Epicurus' Ethical Theory:
The Pleasures of Invulnerability
by Phillip Mitsis

Momentary Monsters: Lucan and His Heroes
by W. R. Johnson

Odysseus Polutropos:
Intertextual Readings in the *Odyssey* and the *Iliad*
by Pietro Pucci

Seneca's *Hercules Furens*:
A Critical Text with Introduction and Commentary
by John G. Fitch

The Rhetoric of Imitation: Genre and Poetic Memory
in Virgil and Other Latin Poets
by Gian Biagio Conte, edited by Charles Segal

Epicurus' Scientific Method
by Elizabeth Asmis

From Myth to Icon:
Reflections of Greek Ethical Doctrine in Literature and Art
by Helen F. North

THE TOWNSEND LECTURES

Artifices of Eternity: Horace's Fourth Book of Odes
by Michael C. J. Putnam

A POETICS OF

Transformation

Prudentius and
Classical Mythology

MARTHA A. MALAMUD

Cornell University Press

ITHACA AND LONDON

First published 1989 by Cornell University Press.

International Standard Book Number 0-8014-2249-3
Library of Congress Catalog Card Number 88-43290
Printed in the United States of America
*Librarians: Library of Congress cataloging information
appears on the last page of the book.*

*The paper in this book is acid-free and meets the guidelines for
permanence and durability of the Committee on Production Guidelines
for Book Longevity of the Council on Library Resources.*

For Bill, Camille, and Mary Malamud

Contents

Acknowledgments

I thank the Graduate School of Cornell University for support during the preliminary stages of this book, and the University of Southern California and the Andrew W. Mellon Foundation for a fellowship in 1985–86. I also thank my friends and colleagues in the Classics departments of both Cornell University and the University of Southern California for their advice and encouragement. I am especially grateful to the following people: Frederick Ahl, the anonymous readers for Cornell University Press, Anthony J. Boyle, Carolyn Dewald, Allison Dodge, Judith Ginsburg, Barry Goldfarb, Jeffrey Henderson, Patricia Johnson, William Levitan, Margaret Malamud, Donald McGuire, and Winthrop Wetherbee.

MARTHA A. MALAMUD

Los Angeles, California

Note on Texts Used

I have used the Latin text of Maurice Cunningham's edition of Prudentius' *Carmina* (Turnholt, 1966) for quotations, with occasional minor changes in punctuation. Maurice Lavarenne's edition (*Prudence: Oeuvres* [Paris, 1955]) provides useful notes. All translations in the text are mine unless otherwise noted; I have tried to be as literal as possible, but occasionally I have given a free translation in order to render sound patterns and wordplays into English. I have generally used the standard abbreviations for authors and their works listed in the *Oxford Classical Dictionary*. Editions of authors quoted in the text appear in the bibliography under the author's name. Abbreviations of scholarly journals are those used in *L'Année Philologique*.

Abbreviations

Works of Prudentius:

Apoth.	*Apotheosis*
Cath.	*Cathemerinon*
CS	*Contra Symmachum*
Ham.	*Hamartigenia*
Perist.	*Peristephanon*
Praef.	*Praefatio*
Ps.	*Psychomachia*

Other Abbreviations:

AASS	*Acta Sanctorum: Les Petits Bollandistes vies des saints de l'Ancien et du Nouveau Testament.* Ed. Msgr. Paul Guérin. 7th ed. 17 vols. Paris: Bloud & Barrac, 1883.
ANRW	*Aufstieg und Niedergang der römischen Welt: Geschichte und Kultur Roms im Spiegel der neueren Forschung.* Ed. Wolfgang Haase and H. Temporini. Berlin and New York: de Gruyter, 1972– .
CCSL	*Corpus Christianorum. Series Latina*
CIL	*Corpus Inscriptionum Latinarum*
CSEL	*Corpus Scriptorum Ecclesiasticorum Latinorum*
CTh	*Codex Theodosianus*
PG	*Patrologia Cursus Completus. Series Graeca.* Ed. J. P. Migne. 161 vols. Paris: J. P. Migne, 1857–1903.
PL	*Patrologia Cursus Completus. Series Latina.* Ed. J. P. Migne. 221 vols. Paris: J. P. Migne, 1844–65.

A Poetics of Transformation

Introduction

Words run amok in the work of Prudentius. He is beyond baroque. Readers of Latin unfamiliar with the literature of Late Antiquity who pick up the *Peristephanon* or the *Psychomachia* expecting to find the work of a Christian Horace or Vergil (labels frequently attached to Prudentius by despairing critics) are in for a rude awakening. For his poetry is far from classical in the conventional sense, and though it is certainly Christian in subject matter, it offers a vision of a Christian universe that is almost unrecognizable to modern readers. The imagery of his poetry is troubling. As we read, we find ourselves in a place of labyrinthine confusion where travelers who have lost their way wander along steep and winding paths and end up ambushed by highwaymen; a place where grotesque miracles occur with edifying regularity; a place where blood is spilled, teeth and bones are shattered, and bodily parts are cut off with abandon. But above all it is a world ruled by semantic determinism, where historical figures become abstractions, abstractions become characters, and metaphors become realities. Intellectual, intertextual, and informed throughout by Prudentius' strange sardonic humor, this is a world in which characters like Oedipa Maas or Captain Ahab might feel at home.

It is not, however, a world in which most contemporary readers, untrained in deciphering the often elaborate codes of Late Antique literature, will feel at ease. Hence this book,

unskilled style"

which is meant as an introduction to rather than an exhaustive
or conclusive survey of Prudentius' verse. There are good
reasons for avoiding such a project. For although there has
been an explosion of scholarship (much of it excellent) in the
field of Late Antique history, there has been no corresponding
surge of interest in the poetry of the period. It is therefore
difficult to place Prudentius in a coherent *literary* context:
though there is good evidence that he was reading and re-
sponding to the other poets of his day, very little work has
been done on the poetic goals and techniques, critical assumptions, and methods of the writers of this period. Until we have
some clearer idea of the literary context of the late fourth and
early fifth centuries, it will be difficult to write the definitive
book on Prudentius' poetry. I have chosen instead to do a close
reading of several of his texts, mostly from the *Peristephanon*,
to see what can be learned from them about Prudentius' poetic
technique and his poetic project. Any such reading is, of
course, shaped by my assumptions and preconceptions. In this
introduction, therefore, I discuss certain trends in current
scholarship that I believe have been helpful in elucidating
various aspects of Prudentius' poetry.

In his essay "Learning and Imagination,"[1] Peter Brown
criticized what he called the "two-tier" model of religion—the
idea, prevalent since Hume, that the religious beliefs of the
aristocracy and the mob are necessarily different and that the
vulgar beliefs of the many tend to corrupt the high-minded
religiosity of the few. He shows how this unexamined assumption has affected the study of Late Antique history:

> Applied to the study of the religious history of Late Antiquity,
> the "two-tier" model encourages the historian to assume that
> any change in the piety of Late Antique men must have been the
> result of the intrusion into the élites of the Christian Church of
> modes of thought current among the masses; and that these
> changes coincided with massive external events, such as fear and

[1]In Brown, *Society and the Holy in Late Antiquity* (Berkeley and Los Angeles,
1982).

anxiety caused by the barbarian invasions or disorientation caused by mass-conversions to Christianity. Such religious phenomena are deemed to belong to the category of "popular religion." The category of "popular religion" is, by definition, timeless and faceless, because it exhibits modes of thinking that are unintelligible except in terms of failure to be something else— failure through the pressures of anxiety, failure through the absence of the cultural and social preconditions of rational thought, failure through that hard fate that has condemned half of the population of any age, through the accident of gender, to being members of "that timorous and pious sex." (p. 12)

Brown's imaginative model of religion in Late Antiquity resembles a "seamless web" more than a "two-tier" approach. He sees no sharp distinction between the religion of the elite and "popular religion" and suggests that we view the entirety of religious ritual and practice as a mirror of Late Antique social realities. Although this book is a literary study and not a contribution to the study of Late Antique social history, Brown's readjustment of our way of thinking about Late Antique religion is essential. To approach Prudentius' *Peristephanon,* a book of poems in honor of martyred Christians, with the "two-tier" approach to religion as our model would not be helpful. Indeed, it would be detrimental to our understanding of this complex poet if we were to attribute the more bizarre narrative elements in the poems to the accidental intrusion of popular religious beliefs and legends.

Brown goes on to say that just as he sees no gulf between popular and elite religion, so he does not consider the Late Antique world to have been split into opposing pagan and Christian camps. He sees instead a world of men and women who took their classical heritage for granted, no matter what their religious beliefs:

For the men of Late Antiquity, the classical past—and especially the gods who hung so close to them in the planets and in the heavy clusters of the Milky Way—were not yet "the past." It was not an option that could be "revived" or "abandoned"; "applied"

3

or "deemed irrelevant." It was part of the air that men breathed, and it is incautious to assume precipitately that, any more than in classical China or in the Islamic world, this mellow air did not contain most of the elements necessary for continual, healthy respiration. (p. 93)

This is an important point of departure for the study of Prudentius and other Late Antique poets. We must not think of them as poets engaged in an attempt to revive, imitate, or attack pagan literary culture. They wrote, from their point of view, from firmly within a highly developed and articulated literary tradition that stretched back to Homer, and they had the luxury of knowing that, because of the remarkable homogeneity of education in the ancient world, their audience was as steeped in that literature as they were. This enabled them, through the judicious use of literary allusion, quotation, and variation, to write in a language whose economy, depth, and precision is hard for us to grasp today, because so many of its terms are lost to us. To quote Brown's essay once again: "The *ars artium* of Late Antique studies consists in avoiding premature judgment as to the 'unreality' of the classical tradition as it was used by Late Antique men. We frequently find that, even in the most traditionalist circles, the ancient language is being discreetly manipulated to act as an enabling formula, or as a commonly-agreed shorthand with which to sum up and so to render manageable strictly contemporary situations" (p. 92).[2]

The use of traditional language as a kind of enabling formula or shorthand was not, of course, solely a Late Antique phenomenon. It is a long-standing characteristic of Latin and Greek literature. Frederick Ahl, another scholar who disregards traditional categories, has turned his attention to the Latin poets' genius for subtly manipulating language. One of his most significant contributions to the study of Latin literature is an article entitled "The Art of Safe Criticism in Greece

[2]For an analysis of a situation in which Paulinus relies on just this sort of formulaic literary shorthand, see Michael Roberts, "Paulinus Poem 11, Virgil's First Eclogue, and the Limits of *Amicitia*," *TAPhA* 115 (1985):271–282.

and Rome." Though it deals primarily with oratory, its implications for poetry are clear. In it, Ahl shows how ancient
writers and speakers dealt with the delicate and often dangerous task of criticizing the powerful: they developed figured
speech, that is, speech in which "the speaker wishes us to
understand something beyond or something different from
what the superficial meaning of his words suggests."[3] Quintilian describes succinctly what needs to be done:

> quamlibet enim apertum, quod modo et aliter intellegi possit, in
> illos tyrannos bene dixeris, quia periculum tantum, non etiam
> offensa vitatur. Quod si ambiguitate sententiae possit eludi,
> nemo non illi furto favet.

> You can speak well and make open statement against the tyrants
> we were discussing, providing the statement can be understood
> in another way. It is only danger you are trying to avoid, not
> giving offense. If you can slip by through ambiguity of expres-
> sion, there's no one who won't enjoy your verbal burglary.[4]

Figured speech, studied ambiguity, and allusive references
and reminiscences that point the reader toward a conclusion
but do not spell it out became characteristic features of Roman
poetry. Ahl has shown us the extent to which this is true and
thus has helped us avoid simplistic and shallow interpretations
of a literature of great depth and complexity.

The search for hidden meanings can be taken too far, of
course. It is dangerous to suppose, for example, that *all* Latin
poetry is disguised political critique, and it is certainly possible
to read too much into an ambiguous line of verse. And yet it is
important to point out that in the imperial period, poets and
orators did develop the art of veiled speech, already established by centuries of legal and rhetorical training, into a

---

[3]Frederick M. Ahl, "The Art of Safe Criticism in Greece and Rome," *AJPh*
105 (1984):174–208. For ancient evidence, see Quintilian *Inst. Or.* 9.1.13–
14; 9.2.65–67; Demetrius *On Style* 288–289.

[4]Quintilian *Inst. Or.* 9.2.67, Ahl's translation in "The Art of Safe Criticism,"
p. 193.

vehicle that allowed them, when necessary, to express criticism or dissent in a way that would not be openly antagonistic to the emperor. Recent scholarship on Ovid and Vergil suggests that these techniques of allusive critique were being developed even in the "Golden Age" of the Augustan principate.

It does not take more than a cursory glance at the almost Byzantine complexity of the formulaic language of fourth- and fifth-century correspondence to make one realize that the art of veiled and careful speech still flourished in the Late Antique period. Though Prudentius tends to stay away from overtly political issues and current events, we must remember that he was for most of his life an official in the imperial court and thus a man trained to weigh his words with extreme care. We must also bear in mind that, although Prudentius' verse purports to be religious rather than political, it was difficult in the late fourth century to keep religion entirely separate from politics. Thus Prudentius, because of his office and because of his subject matter, was in a position to offend easily; it is not surprising to find him dealing with potentially controversial issues in an oblique and indirect way.

To read Prudentius' poetry, then, we must be alert to the literary and linguistic codes that need to be deciphered. But there are cultural codes to be cracked as well. Prudentius, as we shall see, tends to impose patterns from myth and legend onto the lives of his martyrs. I have found useful the work of the French scholars at the Ecole des Hautes Etudes, and in particular the work of Marcel Detienne, for analyzing this aspect of Prudentius' verse. Detienne uses a modified version of Lévi-Straussian structuralism in his analysis of Greek myth. He has shown convincingly that any analysis of a myth that does not include a careful decipherment of its ethnographic context is not simply inadequate, but also misleading. His *Gardens of Adonis* demolishes J. G. Frazer's famous and widely accepted interpretation of Adonis as a dying god of vegetation and fertility through a careful and elegant decipherment of the role of spices and plants in Greek culture and shows us instead an Adonis who represents a dangerous sexual extreme, seduction outside of marriage, which in Greek thought is allied with sterility and impotence.[5] In the opening pages of *Dionysos Slain*, the sequel to *The Gardens of Adonis*, Detienne explains his methodology and sets out how a structural analysis should proceed:

> In order to define the different planes of signification, the analysis should begin by enlarging the field of mythology to include the totality of information about all the facets of the social, spiritual, and material life of the human group under consideration. For example, the appearance of the myrrh tree in the Greek myth of Adonis presupposes a scrupulous inventory of all the evidence revealing to us the way the Greeks represented myrrh and spices in their relationship to other kinds of plants. This inventory not only leads to a definition of the use of myrrh in sacrificial practice or the function of perfumes in sexual life, but also demands that we pose questions of the ensemble of botanical, medical, ritual, and zoological knowledge through which the Greeks transmit to us their classification systems and whole sections of their symbolic system as well. Levi-Strauss is the one who has taught mythologists that in order to understand the signification of a plant or animal, it is necessary each time to determine precisely which role each culture attributes to that plant or animal within a classification system. Nor should one forget that of all the details about such a plant or animal, a given society retains only certain ones in order to assign them a signifying function, and moreover, that each of these details is able to receive different significations. (p. 8)

Detienne's work, though it does not deal specifically with the Late Antique period, does shed some light on the origins of some of Prudentius' problematic martyrs. Although there would seem to be little connection between the hymns of a Late Antique Christian poet and the myths of Dionysos and Adonis, or the culinary, botanical, and sacrificial codes of the Greeks, we must keep in mind the point Peter Brown makes so

[5]Marcel Detienne, *The Gardens of Adonis: Spices in Greek Mythology*, trans. Janet Lloyd (Sussex, 1977), and *Dionysos Slain*, trans. Mireille Muellner and Leonard Muellner (Baltimore, 1979).

forcefully: the Mediterranean basin, despite centuries of political upheaval and the ebbing and flowing of the fortunes of
various nations and empires, enjoyed remarkable cultural sta-
bility. Brown, quoting Plutarch, calls it a "well-mixed bowl of
myths," and the image is apt. Prudentius is not, by any estima-
tion, a mythographer, but like all men and women of his era,
he speaks and thinks in the classical idom. It is not, therefore,
methodologically unsound to allow the work of Detienne, Vernant, and their colleagues to shed some light on some of the
more obscure corners of Prudentius' narrative. And their
work does illuminate some perplexing points—why, for example, Prudentius conflates the life of Cyprian of Antioch, a
seductive magician converted to Christianity, with the more
sober and well-documented life of Cyprian of Carthage, and
why this hybrid figure is associated with the Candida Massa, a
group of martyrs who meet their fate in a lime pit; or why
Prudentius has his virginal martyr Agnes condemned to a
brothel.

My approach is, then, somewhat eclectic and quite different
from most of the recent work done on Prudentius. This is not
so much because I disagree with the conclusions of other
Prudentian scholars (though I do in some cases) as it is because
I am asking different questions of the text. My questions are
these: In what ways are Prudentius' narratives shaped by the
cultural codes that determined the patterns of classical myth?
What explanations can we find for some of the glaring incongruities in his poems? What are the reasons behind his
often bizarre adaptations of hagiographic tradition? And finally, what poetic devices does he use, and to what extent is his
audience expected to participate in the reading of the poem?

Because the questions are different, the portrait of Prudentius that emerges from these pages is different as well. I find
Prudentius' poetry far more complex and intelligently crafted
than do many of the other scholars who have studied it. It is
difficult verse—dense, dark, and frequently violent—but the
reader who develops some feeling for Prudentius' allusive-
ness, his abstract and often punning use of language, and his

manipulation of his sources, whether literary, mythical, or historic, cannot help but find it fascinating. I hope these essays on the *Peristephanon* will help persuade people to turn to Prudentius' work with enthusiasm rather than with the faintly aggrieved sense of duty that some of his critics display, and to accord it the unbiased reading it deserves.

For Prudentius' poetry is anomalous, paradoxical, and ambiguous. He was well aware that he dwelt in a changing world, and this awareness informs his poetry, which is above all an exploration of the boundary zone, that "place between" that both separates and connects pagan and Christian thought. His poetry abounds in imagery suggesting confusion. Labyrinths, endless wanderings, and twisted side roads that lead nowhere recur in his verse, as do agonizing questions about how to find the right way and the true path. It is difficult to live in the borderlands, and this difficulty may account for some of the strangeness of Prudentius' verse and some of the discomfort it provokes. He has been accused of frigidity—accused, indeed, by C. S. Lewis, a man one would expect to find sympathetic to a Christian poet—and the accusation has a certain validity. Lewis, a sincere and passionate convert, has a good ear for detecting notes that are slightly off key, and there are several such notes in Prudentius' *carmina* (songs). His poems are something more, or perhaps other, than statements of faith. They are analytic examinations of the nature of Christian faith. Prudentius may have been a Christian, but he was also a critical thinker, and when he turns his gaze on the church of his day, he does not always like what he sees. The frigidity Lewis sees in the *Psychomachia* arises from the nature of the poem, which is abstract and conceptual; its characters are unbelievable because they are not really characters at all. The *Psychomachia* as a statement of Christian faith is, as many of its critics have pointed out, not terribly convincing. It is extremely unlikely that its purpose was to win converts from the pagan aristocracy through a judicious use of Vergilian allusions, as some of Prudentius' critics seem to believe; it is not a winning poem in any sense. It is, instead, an experimental exploration of an uncertain space, a poem unfolding in a realm outside of history and pushing language to the very limits of meaning. It is not a comfortable space to inhabit; it is not a comforting poem.

There is a radical disjunction, it seems to me, between Prudentius' belief in Christ and his intellectual understanding of the world. His poetry is in a constant state of tension, a tension that expresses itself in extreme violence and that is reflected in the frequent conflict between the text and the subtext. The surface meaning of Prudentius' verse is often undercut by another level of meaning communicated to us not by the narrative but by puns, plays on words, allusions to other texts, and imagery.

I hope in the chapters that follow to expose this other network of signification through a series of close readings of the text of several poems from the *Peristephanon*. But to give the reader unfamiliar with Prudentius and his times some bearings, I provide a brief historical background in Chapter 1 and illustrate in Chapter 2 some features of Latin poetic technique which readers of Prudentius' verse should bear in mind. I begin this second chapter with some general observations about wordplay in classical Latin poetry, with examples from Lucretius and Vergil, and then consider some of the characteristics of fourth-century poetics which can be observed in the works of Ausonius, Optatian, and Prudentius himself. The remaining chapters look briefly at Prudentius' most famous work, the *Psychomachia,* and then at three hymns from the *Peristephanon* dedicated to the martyrs Hippolytus, Cyprian, and Agnes.

I would like in this book to supplement and, to some extent, to change the focus of the work that has already been done on Prudentius' poetry. If I spend less time on Prudentius' Christian beliefs and on his imitations of classical poets than seems appropriate, it is because these aspects of his work have already been well documented by such scholars as Nugent, Gnilka, Witke, Smith, and Fontaine.[6] This study is different,

[6]S. Georgia Nugent, "Vice and Virtue in Allegory: Reading Prudentius' *Psychomachia,*" diss., Cornell University, 1980, and *Allegory and Poetics: The*

both in emphasis and in approach. It wanders down the twisting side roads so often mentioned by our poet, to arrive at a destination different from that reached by other scholars. Some will not find the final destination to their liking; they may yet derive some amusement from the journey.

Structure and Imagery of Prudentius' "Psychomachia" (Frankfurt, 1985); Christian Gnilka, *Studien zur "Psychomachie" des Prudentius* (Wiesbaden, 1963); Jacques Fontaine, *Etudes sur la poésie latine tardive d'Ausone à Prudence* (Paris, 1980), and *Naissance de la poésie latine dans l'occident chrétien: Esquisse d'une historie de la poésie chrétienne du IIIe au VIe siècle* (Paris, 1981); Macklin Smith, *Prudentius' "Psychomachia": A Reexamination* (Princeton, N.J., 1976); Charles Witke, *Numen Litterarum: The Old and the New in Latin Poetry from Constantine to Gregory the Great* (Leiden, 1971).

1

Backgrounds

Prudentius appears from time to time as a character in his poems, and he has left us an autobiographical preface, perhaps to an edition of his collected works.[1] But the preface is, in its way, curiously uninformative, more a Horatian meditation on the passage of time than a self-portrait. From it we learn some facts, which we can put together with details from the other poems to come up with a rough sketch of Prudentius' life, but we get very little idea of the man himself.[2]

Certain facts are known. Aurelius Prudentius Clemens was born in Spain, probably in the town of Calagurris on the Ebro River, in 348 and died sometime after 405, the year in which he issued his collected works. From the preface we know that he was a high official during the reign of Theodosius, who assembled a number of prominent Spaniards together in his court.[3]

[1] I take this preface to be programmatic and assume it was meant to introduce his collected poems, but I agree with Alan Cameron's speculation that Prudentius' poems circulated individually before the collected works were published. See Alan Cameron, *Claudian: Poetry and Propaganda at the Court of Honorius* (Oxford, 1970), app. B.

[2] Italo Lana's *Due capitoli prudenziani: La biografia, la cronologia delle opere, la poetica,* Verba Seniorum, collana di testi e studi patristici, n.s. 2 (Rome, 1962), is the best biographical treatment of Prudentius and does as much as can be done with the facts. Lana also deals competently with the chronology of Prudentius' poems.

[3] John Matthews, *Western Aristocracies and the Imperial Court: A.D. 364–425* (Oxford, 1975), pp. 132–136, has an excellent discussion of the influential circle of Spaniards Theodosius brought with him to Constantinople.

He went into government service after the standard legal and rhetorical training of his day. He says he governed two cities, but we do not know which cities they were. (Siscia, in Yugoslavia, has been suggested as one, but there is no evidence to prove it.) Prudentius retired from politics in his late fifties, and published his book in 405, at the age of fifty-seven.

So much for the information he gives us in the *Praefatio,* the preface to his works. From his other poems we know that he was familiar with Rome and probably traveled a good deal during his career. He was in contact with other poets of his time—Charlet has demonstrated the influence of Ausonius on his poetry;[4] Alan Cameron has discussed the evidence of mutual borrowing between Prudentius and his younger contemporary, the highly political court poet Claudian;[5] and some see possible contacts with the literary but retiring Saint Paulinus of Nola.[6] Prudentius was also familiar with the hymns of Ambrose and the epigrams of Pope Damasus, as we know from the hymns of the *Peristephanon.*

Thus from the scant information we have, we get the impression of a man fully engaged with his times: well traveled, well read, and well connected. He was experienced in court politics and in provincial government; and as familiar with the new Christian poetry of Damasus, Ambrose, and Paulinus as with the more traditional classicizing poetry of Claudian and Ausonius. (The latter two, like Prudentius, were much involved with the politics of the imperial court, Ausonius attaining a position of considerable power as the emperor Gratian's tutor, and Claudian playing the part of propagandist for the

[4]J. L. Charlet, "L'influence d'Ausone sur la poésie de Prudence," diss., Sorbonne (Paris, 1972).

[5]Cameron, *Claudian,* app. B.

[6]Jacques Fontaine, "La poésie comme art spirituel: Les projets poétiques de Paulin et Prudence," in *Naissance de la poésie latine dans l'occident chrétien: Esquisse d'une histoire de la poésie chrétienne du IIIe au VIe siècle* (Paris, 1981), pp. 143–160, and "Société et culture chrétiennes sur l'aire circumpyrénéenne au siècle de Théodose," in *Etudes sur la poésie latine tardive d'Ausone à Prudence* (Paris, 1980), pp. 267–308, and S. Costanza, "Rapporti letterari tra Paolino e Prudenzio," in *Atti del Convegno 31 cinquantenario della morte di S. Paolino di Nola (431–1981),* Nola, Mar. 20–21, 1982 (Rome, 1983).

powerful Stilicho, who essentially acted as regent for Theodosius' son Honorius.)

We tend to think of the Late Antique period as a time of
relentless pursuit of self. Augustine, of course, is the most
famous of the Late Antique explorers of the inner world, but
though the *Confessions* remains the masterpiece of the period
and of the genre, Augustine was not alone in his attempts to
confront the self. The inner lives of Jerome and Paulinus of
Nola shine through their writings, and even a man of affairs
with as little interest in the spiritual as Ausonius has left us
what amounts to a self-portrait in his letters and poems. We
see his family and friends, his connections at court, his friendship with Paulinus, his affection for his little slave girl—in
short, a highly personal world centered around human relationships. As Peter Brown put it, in Late Antiquity "we are
dealing with men who have turned their backs on the towering
order of the universe to seek reassurance in the tight web of
known human relationships: and they have done this in part
because, against this immemorial backdrop, they have, for
good or ill, turned to discover themselves."[7]

But was this a universal tendency in Late Antiquity? In an
age of conversion, confession, and public exploration of the
self, there were men who chose not to bare their souls. Among
them were Prudentius and his younger contemporary Claudian (today competitors for the dubious honor of being called
the "last classical poet"). While Augustine bared his soul to his
God and his public, and Ausonius arranged a civilized portrait
of himself and his family for posterity, Prudentius and Claudian retained the inscrutable mask of the classical poet, keeping their families, friends, and "dark nights of the soul" strictly
to themselves. Self-scrutiny, confession, and even biography
were not the subject of poetry to these writers. This is not to
say that they lacked either self-knowledge or emotion, but
rather that their intellects, their analytic powers, and their
poetic skills were focused elsewhere. We find Claudian turn-

[7]Brown, *The Cult of the Saints: Its Rise and Function in Latin Christianity*
(Chicago, 1981), p. 68.

ing his sharp, sardonic, and outspokenly propagandistic gaze on the spectacle of the political world, while Prudentius looked beyond the human world to a more abstract and intellectualized world of ideas, ideals, and ideologies. Thus Prudentius, like Claudian, might strike the modern reader as slightly anomalous or as one who fails to share in the characteristic tendencies of his age. But the late fourth century was at least as determinedly conservative as it was essentially innovative, and it may be only from our perspective that Prudentius seems to swim against the literary current of his own period.

Imperial Politics

Prudentius lived in a turbulent time. The Roman Empire was under great strain throughout the fourth century, both internally and externally. There was constant warfare, as barbarian tribes tested the strength of the borders in the north and the Persian Empire pressed from the east. Rome was no longer the heart of the civilized world. Troubles in the East forced Constantine to create a new capital, Constantinople, in the early part of the century, and the emperors in the West were on the move patrolling the dangerous frontiers of Gaul and Northern Italy. Within the empire there were serious economic problems—taxation and inflation were cripplingly high. And, perhaps most relevant to our study of Prudentius, the relationship between religion and the state was undergoing a radical transformation. The conversion of Constantine had enormous ramifications for both the government and the Catholic church, starting a process that would, by the beginning of the fifth century, redefine both institutions.

Prudentius' life spanned the last half of the fourth century, the years when Constantine's legacy to history began to be felt.[8] He was born in 348, only six years before Augustine, his

[8]My treatment of the historic background is necessarily brief and extremely schematic. Readers unfamiliar with the period are urged to turn to the works of W. H. C. Frend, Peter Brown, and John Matthews.

more famous contemporary and the man whose towering presence has shaped our perception of the fourth century. Though Christianity rapidly gained in popularity throughout the empire once it had been embraced by Constantine and his successors, it was not yet the official religion of the empire. Indeed, the new religion could have suffered a serious blow in 361, when the pagan emperor Julian came to the throne and used his influence and resources to encourage a revival of the Roman state religion and a suppression of Christianity. Julian's most potentially damaging blow against Christianity was his passage of a law requiring teachers of rhetoric and literature to return to the old religion or give up teaching—an edict even Ammianus Marcellinus found *inclemens* (Amm. Marcel. 22.10). Julian's reign was brief, however; he died in battle in 363. His successors, Jovian (who died shortly after Julian) and Valentinian (who was made emperor in Nicaea in 364 and divided the empire with his brother Valens, Valentinian taking the West) were Christian, and Julian's attempt to reverse the Christianization of the empire was ended.

Valentinian, an emperor with a military background, turned his attention to securing the Western provinces, and in so doing managed to alienate the senatorial class in Rome by turning traditionally senatorial offices over to newcomers from the imperial bureaucracy and, later in his reign, by prosecuting a number of prominent senators for treason and sorcery.[9] In 367 Valentinian settled his court at Trier, a place Matthews characterizes as "an environment, the essence of which was in its fluidity, and in its comparative lack of regional prejudices."[10] Indeed, in this fluid environment we find such disparate types as Jerome, who was just beginning his career; Ausonius, the influential poet from Gaul who became the tutor of Valentinian's son Gratian; and the charismatic bishop Martin of Tours. The atmosphere at Valentinian's court was religiously orthodox, but at the same time a man like Ausonius, whose adherence to Christianity was nominal, could thrive by

[9]See Matthews, *Western Aristocracies*, pp. 38–55.
[10]Ibid., p. 48.

means of his command of classical literature and learning and could please the emperor by the composition of his notorious *Cento Nuptialis,* an obscene epithalamium made up of lines and half-lines from Vergil. It is important to keep in mind that the steady advance of Christianity by no means eliminated toleration of, and indeed appreciation for, classical education.

Valentinian died in 375 and was succeeded in the West by Gratian, an event that brought Ausonius into a very prominent position. Under Gratian the hostility between the senatorial class in Rome and the court was mitigated, and the provincial professional bureaucrats from Valentinian's entourage were replaced by men from Western aristocratic families. The relative harmony of Gratian's reign was to be short-lived, however. The Eastern emperor, Valens, was killed in the devastating defeat by the Visigoths at Adrianople in 378 and was succeeded in 379 by the young Theodosius, who had been living in Spain in retirement after the political downfall and death of his father.

Theodosius spent the early part of his reign campaigning against the Goths and eventually negotiated a treaty permitting the Goths to settle on the other side of the Danube. But while Theodosius moved vigorously in the East and took up residence in Constantinople, affairs in the West were far from settled. Gratian's regime was threatened by the usurper Maximus, who invaded Gaul in 383, while Gratian was in northern Italy preparing a campaign against the Alamanni. In August of that year Gratian was killed by Maximus' general Andragathius and succeeded by the child Valentinian II.

For the next four years there were three imperial courts— Maximus controlling Spain and Gaul from Trier, Theodosius ruling the East from Constantinople, and Valentinian II and his supporters clinging to their positions in Milan. This uneasy balance of power lasted until Maximus invaded Italy in 387 and drove the young emperor's court out of Milan. Valentinian then traveled to Thessalonica to seek protection from Theodosius, whose armies soon moved decisively against Maximus, defeating and killing him in August of 388.

Theodosius remained in Italy for the next two years, attempting to stabilize the Western half of the empire. During this time he twice came into conflict with Ambrose, the influential bishop of Milan. It is a mark of the changing relationship between the emperor and the church that Ambrose won both battles. The first case concerned the burning of a synagogue and of a heretic chapel in the town of Callinicum by an angry mob incited by their bishop. Theodosius at first demanded that the bishop pay for the restoration of the synagogue, an attitude consistent with normal governmental response to riots, but inconsistent with Theodosius' own supporters' evangelistic policy of closing down non-Christian places of worship. Ambrose, refusing to take communion until Theodosius changed his mind and appealing directly to his congregation, forced Theodosius to revoke his order for the restoration of the synagogue. In the second case, Ambrose threatened the emperor with excommunication if he did not do penance for a massacre in Thessalonica, which Theodosius had ordered in response to the murder of a military commander in that city. Once again Theodosius gave in to the bishop. It is, as Matthews says, not surprising that after this experience with Ambrose Theodosius in 391 passed his edict barring all forms of pagan sacrifices and access to pagan temples.[11]

Later in 391, Theodosius returned to Constantinople, but the situation in the West was still not settled. In 392, the depressed and essentially powerless Valentinian II died, apparently by suicide, opening the way for yet another struggle for the Western throne. Propelled by the powerful general Arbogastes, Eugenius, a former teacher of rhetoric, took the throne. Although Eugenius was a Christian, his rebellion took on the appearance of a pagan reaction against Theodosius, mostly because of the actions of Eugenius' supporter, the praetorian prefect Nicomachus Flavianus, who restored a

[11]For a thorough discussion of Theodosius' time in Italy and his experiences with Ambrose, see Matthews, *Western Aristocracies*, pp. 229–238, which I have summarized here.

number of pagan temples and religious festivals in Rome. In 394, Theodosius put an end to the revolt, defeating Eugenius in the famous battle of the Frigidus, and eliminating any possibility of a "pagan revolution."[12] In the winter of that year, Theodosius, who had returned once more to the court at Milan, grew ill and died, leaving the empire to his two young sons, Honorius and Arcadius.

The Supporters of Theodosius

What was Prudentius doing during these tempestuous years? Where did he fit into the complicated political situation? It is likely that he was among the group of Spaniards who benefited from the accession of Theodosius; certainly he rose to high office during Theodosius' reign. Prudentius, however, is essentially silent on the subject of his political career, saying only that he was close to the emperor and the governor of two cities:

> bis legum moderamine
> > frenos nobilium reximus urbium,
> > ius civile bonis reddidimus, terruimus reos.
> tandem militiae gradu
> > evectum pietas principis extulit
> > adsumptum propius stare iubens ordine proximo.
> > > *(Praef.* 16–21)

Twice I guided the course of noble cities and checked them with the curb of law. I gave justice to the good and terrified the guilty. Finally the loyalty of the emperor carried me up the ladder of office, bidding me to stand closer to him in the nearest rank.

Which cities Prudentius governed and what position he had in the bureaucracy are unclear. His career seems to follow the

[12]See Matthews, "The Historical Setting of the *Carmen contra Paganos* (*Cod. Par. Lat.* 8084)," *Historia* 20 (1970):464–479.

pattern set by other Spanish and Gallic officials who came to power with Theodosius and who had such an impact on imperial policy in the East when they arrived in Constantinople. The men Theodosius brought with him to the East were characterized by a combination of rigid orthodox piety and evangelical zeal. High on their agenda were the elimination of paganism and the suppression of heresy within the empire, and they used the apparatus of government to enforce their program. These men included Nebridius, the city prefect of Constantinople in 386;[13] Nummius Aemilianus Dexter, whose father was Pacianus, the bishop of Constantinople, and to whom Jerome dedicated his *De viris illustribus;* and Maternus Cynegius, the praetorian prefect of the East from 284–288, who "devoted himself to an aggressive pilgrimage of violence" through the Eastern half of the empire, destroying pagan temples and monuments.[14] One of this group, though not a Spaniard, is Flavius Rufinus, Theodosius' minister and strongman, the villain of Claudian's invective *In Rufinum,* who, as we shall see later, was assassinated by the army only nineteen days after Theodosius' burial.[15] We have a fairly good picture of these supporters of Theodosius:

> Under Theodosius, it was for [the Spanish aristocracy] to win advancement and impose themselves upon the provinces of the eastern empire. The Spaniards appear . . . to stand for the ideals of a new and eager Christian piety, as they contribute their efforts to the enforcement of western orthodoxy in the east, and make their personal connections in the world of eastern asceticism. (Matthews, *Western Aristocracies,* p. 146)

The Spanish upper classes were, by the late fourth century, largely Christianized, and indeed by Prudentius' day there was already a tradition of Spanish contributions to Christian litera-

[13]Jerome *Ep.* 79.1.
[14]Matthews, *Western Aristocracies,* p. 140.
[15]Rufinus was from southwestern Gaul, a region with close ties to Spain. For a discussion of this environment, see Fontaine, "Société et culture chrétiennes."

ture.[16] Although there is little direct evidence regarding the progress of Christianity in Spain at this time, it does seem that Spain, like southern Gaul, was home to ascetic, evangelical movements, as the rapid spread and stubborn persistence of the Priscillian heresy suggests.[17] Certainly the Spanish and Gallic members of Theodosius' entourage were known for their personal piety, and particularly for their devotion to the cult of the martyrs. And Theodosius himself was remarkable not only for his own religious enthusiasm, but also for his use of secular power for religious ends. He was, in Matthews' words, "an emperor responsive to ecclesiastical pressures, actively promoting piety by his personal example and that of his court, suppressing heresy and paganism by legislation and enforcement."[18] In 380, he issued an edict demanding that all the peoples of the empire adhere to a strictly Western orthodox form of Christianity,[19] and in 391 he banned all pagan sacrifices and prohibited access to pagan temples.[20]

Although Prudentius clearly approved of Theodosius, although he ascribes his successful career to Theodosius in his preface, and although he is from Spain, where Theodosius formed his closest connections, it is perhaps too much to assume he was one of the orthodox insiders who enforced and encouraged Theodosius' evangelistic policies. While he praises Theodosius' edict banning pagan worship in the *Contra Symmachum* 1, he implicitly rebukes the religious extremists who went about destroying pagan temples and works of art by putting a speech in the emperor's mouth which calls for tolera-

[16]See Matthews, *Western Aristocracies*, p. 147, for a brief discussion of Spanish literary figures in the late empire. Aside from Prudentius, he mentions Acilius Severus, who was included in Jerome's *De viris illustribus;* a relative of Severus who wrote an autobiography in mixed prose and verse; and Iuvencus, who converted the four gospels into hexameters.

[17]See Henry Chadwick, *Priscillian of Avila: The Occult and the Charismatic in the Early Church* (New York and London, 1976); Aline Rousselle, "Quelques Aspectes de l'affaire Priscillianiste," *REA* 83 (1981):85–96; and W. H. C. Frend, *The Rise of Christianity* (London, 1984), pp. 711–715.

[18]Matthews, *Western Aristocracies*, p. 99.

[19]*CTh*. 16.1.2.

[20]*CTh* 16.10.10.

tion of sorts—the statues may remain, as long as they are no longer worshipped:

> liceat statuas consistere puras,
> artificum magnorum opera: hae pulcherrima nostrae
> ornamenta fiant patriae, nec decolor usus
> in vitium versae monumenta coinquinet artis.
>
> (*CS* 1.502–505)

Let the statues, the work of great artists, stand clean: let them be our country's loveliest ornament, and let no tainted usage steep the monuments of converted art in sin.

This plea for preservation of pagan statues as works of art is in stark contrast to the attitude of other Spanish officials of Theodosius, such as the prefect Maternus Cynegius, who cut a swath through the East, destroying pagan monuments in Edessa, Apamea, and Egypt.[21]

Indeed, though Prudentius seems at first a likely candidate for membership in the orthodox Spanish circles of Theodosius' court, there are other indications that he was not entirely comfortable with their brand of piety. He sides, for example, with the court poet Claudian, who condemned Theodosius' orthodox strongman Rufinus: as we shall see, Prudentius' description of the dismemberment and death of Discordia/ Heresy in the *Psychomachia* is similar to Claudian's account of Rufinus' death and contains a clear verbal echo of Claudian's verse.[22] Furthermore, his friendly treatment of Symmachus, who is characterized throughout the *Contra Symmachum* with extreme courtesy, and his enthusiastic borrowing from contemporary poets whose Christianity is dubious at best, such as Claudian and Ausonius, suggest he was at least willing to engage in a dialogue with them. Finally, as I will demonstrate throughout the remainder of this book, Prudentius' attitude

---

[21]Matthews, *Western Aristocracies*, pp. 140–142, 232–233, for a description of Cynegius' activities and a list of sources.

[22]See Cameron, *Claudian*, app. B, p. 472. Prudentius echoes a verse from *Ruf* 2.382 in *Psych.* 736.

toward the pagan classics is not purely adversarial. His poetry may be Christian in subject matter, but he writes from within the classical tradition.

Despite the tensions between pagans and Christians in the late fourth century, exacerbated by the religious policy of Theodosius and his sons, we must not be too quick to assume they were separated by an unbridgeable gulf. Pagans and Christians shared a common heritage, *pace* Jerome, in classical culture. There was, as Peter Brown puts it, "an unexplored borderline between the pagan and Christian culture of Rome," and nowhere is that liminal area more apparent than in the literature of the age.[23] The Vergilian cento of Proba, which patches together Vergilian lines and half-lines to tell the story of the birth of Christ, is the most frequently cited example of Christian acceptance—indeed, Christian appropriation—of classical form.[24] Even Paulinus of Nola, despite his renunciation of the secular world, celebrates the birthday of Saint Felix each year in classical meters and is willing to concede the possibility of pagan virtue.[25]

There is also the curious example of Ausonius, who, though nominally a Christian, seems indifferent to religion. He wrote one of the more remarkable poems of the fourth century, *Cupid Crucified.* It would be fascinating as a literary document for its elaborate frame even if its subject matter were devoid of interest, for Ausonius has set it up as if it were a Russian doll that opens to reveal another, smaller doll inside. The poem is constructed as follows: Ausonius writes a letter to a friend in which he encloses a poem he has written about a painting of a dream about, among other things, ghosts. In the dream, the

[23]Brown, *World of Late Antiquity,* p. 178.

[24]Elizabeth A. Clark and Diane Hatch, *The Golden Bough, the Oaken Cross: The Vergilian Cento of Faltonia Betitia Proba* (Chico, Calif., 1981).

[25]Paulinus, *Carm.* 21.230–238. "tamen in tenebris inpiarum mentium / lucis videmus emicasse semina / in tempore ipso noctis antiquae sitis, / quibus probata quamlibet gentilibus / mens et voluntas lege naturae fuit" (And yet, in the shadows of the minds of unbelievers, we see that seeds of light have shone forth even in those who lived in that time of ancient darkness. To them, though they were gentiles, the law of nature gave the proper mind and will." Peter Brown, *The World of Late Antiquity,* p. 179, mentions this passage.

god Cupid finds himself on trial in the underworld, and his judges are the tragic heroines of classical poetry who suffered for love. He is convicted and sentenced to die, but he wakes up before the sentence is carried out. This is a clear and unusually elaborate example of a pagan treatment of a Christian theme (the god of love crucified): the story of Christ is transformed to fit into the framework of classical mythology.

Ausonius is not being entirely original here; though there are no similar equations between Cupid and Christ in literature, there are lamps from Gaul decorated with scenes of Cupids suffering various tortures in the arena.[26] Clearly there was room for overlapping treatments of religious ideas and artistic and literary themes in the Late Antique period. Whatever the theological and ideological differences between pagans and Christians, they share a common cultural heritage and a common language. The gap between Christian and classical cultures may, as has been argued, have been at its widest in the Western empire in the late fourth century, but the relationship between the two was nevertheless symbiotic.[27] We can see the same process of adaptation working in Paulinus, Prudentius, and Iuvencus, who frequently use Vergilian epithets for Jupiter to describe the Christian God, and in tomb paintings and sarcophagi, where Christian artists drew heavily on pagan symbols of the afterlife and where pagan and Christian motifs sometimes appear side by side.[28]

[26]J. W. Salomonson, *Voluptatem spectandi non perdat sed mutet: Observations sur l'iconographie du martyre en Afrique romaine* (Amsterdam, 1979).

[27]R. A. Markus, "Paganism, Christianity and the Latin Classics in the Fourth Century," in *From Augustine to Gregory the Great* (London, 1983), sees the last half of the fourth century as a time of extreme tension between pagans and Christians: "Jerome, Augustine, Prudentius, and Orosius belong to the world of Praetextatus, the Symmachi and the Flaviani: a world in which the age-old tensions between paganism and Christianity were once again as sharply crystallised as they were never again to be. These decades opened a real possibility of a brutal rejection of the whole classical past by a triumphantly aggressive Catholicism." While Markus is correct to point out the tensions of the period, I find the notion of a "brutal rejection of the whole classical past" unlikely at this date.

[28]The Via Latina catacomb, for example, contains paintings of Heracles, Alcestis, and the death of Cleopatra along with standard Christian portrayals

Prudentius, a sincere if perhaps uncomfortable Christian and most probably an admirer of Theodosius, nevertheless stands with one foot in this cultural no-man's-land. His subject matter is relentlessly Christian, but his form is traditional, and this reliance on the Roman literary tradition extends beyond his metrics into the conceptual framework of his poetry. He occupies a unique space in the history of literature, for his poetry is radically different from later Christian verse, even from the work of the later medieval poets who admired and attempted to imitate him. Despite his popularity (we know from Sidonius that he was a "classic" by the sixth century), Prudentius' complexity and ambiguity, qualities he shared with Claudian and Ausonius, were seldom successfully imitated. Christian literature moved off along the path marked by Ambrose, Paulinus, and Augustine; Prudentius' work remained a lonely and cryptic monument at the crossroads of history.

---

of biblical characters. See Antonio Ferrua, *Le pitture della Nuova Catacomba di Via Latina*, Monumenta di Antichità Cristiana II Serie (Vatican City, 1960).

2

Word Games

The extent to which classical poets depended on puns and etymological wordplay has received some discussion recently, most notably by Jane Snyder in her book *Puns and Poetry in Lucretius' "De Rerum Natura"* and by Frederick M. Ahl in his *Metaformations.*[1] Prudentius and most of his poetic contemporaries were particularly fond of wordplay and adept in various sorts of verbal manipulations. For the reader unfamiliar with this aspect of Latin verse, I begin this chapter with a brief discussion of this sort of wordplay in Lucretius and in Vergil.

Lucretius is, in many ways, the easiest of the Latin poets to deal with, at least with regard to the connection between verbal play and sense in his verse. Lucretius set out to create a poem that was at the same time an epic and a scientific model of Epicurean theory, and he is quite explicit about his poetic theory and its relationship to his subject matter. In the first two books of the *De rerum natura*, Lucretius five times draws an analogy between his verse and the atomic structure of the universe, comparing the *primordia rerum*, the "first beginnings" of things which make up all matter, to the letters of the alphabet which make up all the words in his poem. This repetition is

---

[1]Snyder, *Puns and Poetry in Lucretius' "De Rerum Natura"* (Amsterdam, 1980); Ahl, *Metaformations: Soundplay and Wordplay in Ovid and Other Classical Poets* (Ithaca, N.Y., 1985); Eva M. Thury, "Lucretius' Poem as a *Simulacrum* of the *Rerum Natura*," *AJP* 108 (1987):270–294.

significant: the poet clearly does not want his readers to miss his point. This set of analogies is, in effect, a blueprint to the poem. Lucretius is alerting his readers to the proper way to read his verse. Jane Snyder has analyzed these passages in detail in her book. I will look briefly at only one of them to give the reader an idea of Lucretius' style.

In the following passage from *De rerum natura* 1, Lucretius not only compares the atoms that make up all matter to the letters of the alphabet, but also explicitly uses his own verses as an analogy:

> nimirum quia multa modis communia multis
> multarum rerum in rebus primordia mixta
> sunt, ideo variis variae res rebus aluntur.
> atque eadem magni refert primordia saepe
> cum quibus et quali positura contineantur
> et quos inter se dent motus accipiantque;
> namque eadem caelum mare terras flumina solem
> constituunt, eadem fruges arbusta animantis,
> verum aliis alioque modo commixta moventur.
> quin etiam passim nostris in versibus ipsis
> multa elementa vides multis communia verbis,
> cum tamen inter se versus ac verba necesse est
> confiteare et re et sonitu distare sonanti.
> tantum elementa queunt permutato ordine solo;
> at rerum quae sunt primordia, plura adhibere
> possunt unde queant variae res quaeque creari.
>
> (*DRN* 1.814–829)

Certainly since many atoms common to many things in many ways are mixed in things, then many things are nourished by various others. And it often makes a big difference with what and in what positions these atoms are held together and what sort of movements they give and receive among themselves. For the same atoms make up the sky, the sea, the lands, the rivers, the sun; the same make up crops, shrubs, and creatures that breathe, but they move differently, mixed with other atoms and in different ways. Now, you can surely see that everywhere in my verses there are many letters (*elementa*) common to many words, while at the same time you must admit that both the lines and the words differ from each other both in meaning and in the sound of their sounding. You can do this much with letters just by changing their order, but the elements which are the beginnings of things carry other qualities, from which all the various kinds of things can be created.

Lucretius was not the first to draw the analogy between atoms and letters of the alphabet. It may go back as far as Democritus and is a commonplace of Atomistic rhetoric, as Snyder demonstrates.[2] Aristotle uses it in *Metaphysics* 985b, in his discussion of the theories of Democritus and Leucippus:

> For they say that matter differs only in form, contact, and orientation. Of these, form means shape, contact means order, and orientation position. Indeed, A differs from N in shape, AN from NA in order, and Z from N in position. (*Metaphysics* 985b16–19)

Of the possible variations Aristotle mentions (shape, order, and orientation), it is order that most interests Lucretius from a poetic point of view. Shape and orientation are as important for atoms, but as he stresses in the passage quoted above, his verses differ in sound and substance simply because the *order* of the letters is rearranged. As Snyder says,

> it is clear . . . that the poet is not referring to "permutations" of a single word when he says *permutato ordine* (1. 827), but is thinking rather of how one can take the twenty-one letters of the Latin alphabet (or twenty-three, counting y and z) and put a selection of them together in one combination to get one word or can put a slightly different selection of them together to get a different word, as, for example *versus . . . verba* (1. 825) and *sonitu . . . sonanti* (1. 826). The emphasis is on the idea that two given distinct words may both use several of the same letters although the overall combination of letters is different, as is most readily apparent in two words which have one or more common syllables. (pp. 40–41)

[2]See her discussion in *Puns and Poetry*, chap. 2.

Snyder's observations do not exhaust the possibilities of discovering plays on words in these lines. One of Lucretius' best effects comes in line 826: *confiTEaRE ET RE ET sonitu distaRE sonanti,* where the pairs TE and RE flip-flop through the line, changing both meaning and sound according to their new places. This sort of syllabic wordplay is something Lucretius is particularly fond of. He uses it again, more meaningfully, when he comes back to the atoms/letters analogy a little later in Book 1. In this passage he sets out to show that the same sort of atoms are mixed up in many different things, but this time he uses syllabic wordplay to broaden the implications of the analogy:

> iamne vides igitur, paulo quod diximus ante,
> permagni referre eadem primordia saepe
> cum quibus et quali positura contineantur
> et quos inter se dent motus accipiantque,
> atque eadem paulo inter se mutata creare
> ignes et lignum? quo pacto verba quoque ipsa
> inter se paulo mutatis sunt elementis,
> cum ligna atque ignes distincta voce notemus.

(DRN 1.907–913)

Now do you see, as I said shortly before, that it often makes a big difference with what and in what positions these atoms are held together, and what sort of movements they exchange among themselves, and how the same atoms slightly changed among themselves create fire and wood (*ignes et lignum*)? In the same way the words themselves also consist of elements slightly changed among themselves, as when we mark wood and fire with different sounds.

Here Lucretius' punning goes beyond simple repetition and variation in the order of sounds and letters. Just as the presence of the same elements in apparently different substances points to an underlying atomic similarity, so, his example seems to assert, the presence of the same letters in different words points to an underlying similarity of sense. Lucretius chooses an economical example: fire (*ignis*) and wood (*lignum*) are not identical, but they are composed of similar elements slightly rearranged. The words themselves form a model for Lucretius' reader to contemplate, for the word for wood, *lIG-Num*, contains within it the root of the word for fire (IGN).[3]

Lucretius' verse is a microcosmic model of the atomic universe. His language mirrors as closely as possible the laws he sees operating in the physical world—hence his fascination with puns, anagrammatic wordplays, alliteration, rhyme, and repetition, repetition not only of sounds and words, but of entire lines or passages. Letters, syllables, words, phrases, and larger segments of verse are Lucretius' building blocks, which he deliberately combines and recombines to imitate the ceaseless motion of atoms in the void. Yet as the *ignes et lignum* example illustrates, Lucretius does not give up all claims of order for his own verse, however willing he may be to contemplate the randomness of the universe. His verse is order imitating chaos; the random joinings of the atoms are mimicked by the poet's significant combinations of letters and syllables.[4]

Though Lucretius is unusually explicit in his discussion of his poetic technique, he is not the only Latin poet to take an interest in wordplay. Vergil is extremely fond of puns and etymologies, particularly of proper names. When, in *Aeneid* 7.767, he mentions the twice-born Hippolytus, he follows the Greek name with a Latin "translation": *Hippolytus, distractus equis* ("Hippolytus, torn apart by horses"). And in the famous opening passage of *Aeneid* 1, he makes it ironically clear in the words *urbs antiqua fuit*, referring to Carthage, that he knew *Carthago* in Punic meant "new city."[5] Wordplays abound in

---

[3]Lucretius' choice of a model here may have a significance beyond the similarity of the two words' sounds. *Lignum* translates the Greek word *hule*, "wood," which is also the term the Greeks used for "matter," the basic stuff of the universe. The principle Lucretius is setting forth here applies not simply to wood and fire, but to all matter.

[4]See, for example, Snyder's discussion of Lucretius' series of verbal plays on *mater, terra,* and *materies,* in her *Puns and Poetry,* pp. 93–94.

[5]Servius at *Aen.* 1.366 comments: *Carthago est lingua Poenorum nova civitas, ut docet Livius* (Carthage, in the language of the Phoenicians, means "New

Vergil. Here, in a short passage from *Aeneid* 10, we can see how his language, like Lucretius', serves as a model for the ideas he is trying to convey:

> vos etiam, gemini, Rutulis cecidistis in arvis,
> Daucia, Laride Thymberque, simillime proles,
> indiscreta suis gratusque parentibus error,
> at nunc dura dedit vobis discrimina Pallas.
> nam tibi, Thymbre, caput Evandrius abstulit ensis;
> te decisa suum, Laride, dextera quaerit
> semianimesque micant digiti ferrumque retractant.
>
> (*Aen.* 10.390–396)

You too, twins, fell together in the Rutulian fields. Larides and Thymber, identical sons of Daucus, you were indistinguishable—a happy source of confusion to your parents. But now Pallas has drawn the hard distinctions of death. Poor Thymber, Evander's son cut off your head with his sword, and Larides, your severed hand seeks its own you, and your half-living fingers flicker and clutch again at the sword.

Here the *topos* of the amputated limb that retains some life is the punch line for a grim joke. The twins, Larides and Thymber, are so much alike that even their parents cannot tell them apart. Only the *dura discrimina,* the "hard distinctions," of death distinguish them in the end: Larides loses his right hand and his brother is decapitated. The flickering fingers of Larides' detached hand, clutching in vain at the sword and searching for their master, have a curious function in the text. The scene is set up with what some would call typical Vergilian pathos—we are introduced to the twins, reminded of their parents' love for them, and seduced by the repeated apostrophes (*gemini,* line 390, *Laride Thymberque,* line 391, and *Laride,* line 395) into a ponderous sentimentality. This picture is undercut at the end by Vergil's sudden shift from the senti-

City," as Livy shows). See Ahl, *Metaformations,* pp. 62–63, for a discussion of these Vergilian wordplays.

mental to the grotesque: an amputated hand with half dead,
flickering fingers forces our attention away from the senti-
mental aspects of the scene and toward the deeper issues of
the poem.[6] The deliberate exaggeration of the macabre lends
an air of bitter mockery to the possibility of noble death on the
battlefield, but even more than that, the various elements of
the scene—the identical twins, the double amputation, and
the life that remains in the dismembered limb—combine with
the language of the passage to direct our attention toward the
fundamental question of identity.

Beneath the polished surface of the poem, Vergil's language reflects confusion of identity, doubling, and uncertainty
about the boundaries of life and death. After the introduction
of the twins, the text generates a series of words with the
notions of likeness, confusion, liminality, and doubleness contained either in their overt meaning or in their component
parts. I should note that I agree with Ahl's conclusion that
verbal play in Latin can occur at the level of the letter and is
not confined to plays on identical sounds—in other words,
difference in vowel quantities does not prevent wordplay. Ahl
cites, for example, Varro's derivation of *solum*, "soil," with a
short *o*, from *solus*, "alone," with a long *o*.[7] In the passage
under scrutiny here, the words suggesting doubleness either
in their meaning or in letter combinations within the words
are: *gemini; dis* in *ceciDIStis, inDIScreta,* and *DIScrimina; sim-
illime; error; bis* in *voBIS;* and *semi* in *SEMIanimesque.* The original confusion between the identities of the twins, a confusion
not even their parents could resolve, is ostensibly "solved" by
the sword of Pallas, but the *dura discrimina,* the "hard distinc-

[6]The phrase *micare digitos* is used to refer to a betting game along the lines
of "Scissors, Paper, Stone." See Cicero *Div.* 2.41.85 and Suetonius *Aug.* 13.

[7]See Ahl, *Metaformations,* pp. 56–57, and Varro *Lingua Latina* 5.22. Not all
of Ahl's rules for Varronian wordplay are necessary for appreciating wordplay in Prudentius, but it seems hard to deny that many Latin poets play with
anagrams, where the vowels have an absolute value. Ahl cites different poets'
plays on *liber* and *libellus,* both with short *i*'s, and *liber* (free), *liberi* (children),
and *libertus* (freedman), all with long *i*'s, as in Ovid *Tristia* 1.1 and Martial's
Epigrams 1.2.1, 7 and 1.70.1. Perhaps the most extreme example of this
tendency is Optatian, for which see below, chap. 2.

tions" (or, if we stress the syllabic content of the phrase, the "twin crimes" of mutilation and death) point to deeper ambiguities than the *gratus error*, the "happy confusion," of identical twins.

Larides' hand seems to move with a will of its own after it has been amputated. Its *anima*, or life force, has not yet left it entirely, and it is somehow possessed of a rudimentary sense of identity—it knows to seek its master. The confusion that results when the hand, which is supposed to be subordinate to the body as a whole, is forced into autonomy, is reflected in the bizarre apostrophe of line 395: *te decisa suum, Laride, dextera quaerit* (Larides, your severed hand seeks its own you). The oddly linked *te . . . suum* emphasizes the unusual relationship between Larides' hand and Larides himself. He, whose similarity to his brother has caused confusion throughout their lives, carries his disturbing tendency to fall between categories with him to his death. Pallas's sword eliminates the happy confusion of identical appearance, but the problem of replication and repetition remains as Larides' hand, like a segment cut from an earthworm, takes on for a moment an autonomous life.

Paradoxically, the sword's harsh distinctions do not, in the end, solve the riddle of the twins' identity. Though the double mutilation apparently makes a permanent distinction between the twins, it is on another level a sign of permanent loss of identity, for the amputation of the head or the hands of a corpse robs it of human identity and is a token of anonymity and absence, the hallmarks of death. Furthermore, it can be argued that the loss of a hand is, in some sense, symbolically equivalent to decapitation, so that even in death the twins retain their symmetrical doubleness. The death of Cicero provides one parallel: after his murder, Antony ordered Cicero's hands and head cut off and nailed to the rostrum—his hands for having written the *Philippics*, and his head because of his oratorical skills.

Vergil's punning, riddling language alerts the reader, here and elsewhere, to levels of meaning beyond the narrative. Later poets, particularly Ovid and Statius, are equally adept at

mastering the subtext; indeed, those poets set about to de-
molish the convention of narrative in their respective epics,
although in different ways. In the *Metamorphoses,* narrative
explodes; the reader is treated to a dizzying succession of
narrators and narrative patterns: themes, motifs, plot elements, phrases, and character types are repeated, with variation, almost infinitely. The *Thebaid* works differently—it gives
the impression of being barely able to spin out its basic plot
line. In a sense, it *implodes;* the plot halts, again and again,
while Statius pauses to scrutinize the main philosophical question of the poem—causality. The destruction of conventional
narrative in poems such as these draws attention away from
plot and toward the poets' use of language. Elements such as
imagery, allusions to other texts, similes, metaphors, etymological wordplays—in short, all the verbal techniques at the
poet's command—are, rather than the plot itself, charged
with carrying the burden of meaning. This tendency to move
away from narrative poetry toward a more abstract literature
requiring the reader's active participation becomes a significant one in Late Antique literature, as the work of Optatian
and Ausonius clearly demonstrates.

Playing by the Rules

Ausonius is perhaps best known for his long correspondence and friendship with the literary but retiring Saint Paulinus of Nola. In addition to his letters to Paulinus, Ausonius
left a collection of curious poetry, which includes riddles, metrical stunt poems, and other oddities. He was in the habit of
prefacing his poems with prose introductions to explain the
circumstances under which they were written and what sort of
metrical or other tricks he used to compose them. In the
introduction to his notorious *Cento nuptialis,* he compares the
poem to a puzzle, which he describes in these words:

> harum verticularum variis coagmentis simulantur species
> mille formarum: helephantus belua aut aper bestia,

anser volans et mirmillo in armis, subsidens venator
et latrans canis, quin et turris et cantharus et alia
huiusmodi innumerabilium figurarum, quae alius alio
scientius variegant. sed peritorum concinnatio
miraculum est, imperitorum iunctura ridiculum.[8]

When these pieces are joined together in various ways, they
imitate the appearance of a thousand forms: a monstrous elephant or a fierce boar; a flying goose or a gladiator in arms; a
seated hunter or a barking dog; even a tower or a drinking cup
or an infinite number of shapes of this sort, which some can put
together more skillfully than others. But the harmony produced
by an experienced player is miraculous, while the arbitrary arrangements of the amateur are ridiculous.

The puzzle to which Ausonius refers was made of pieces of
bones or ivory and was called the *ostomachia,* or "battle of the
bones." It was made of fourteen triangular pieces cut from a
rectangle, which could be assembled and reassembled to form
a variety of shapes: an elephant, a boar, a goose, and so on. At
first glance, it resembles a modern jigsaw puzzle, but though it
is simpler in form than most jigsaw puzzles, it is conceptually
more complicated, for in a jigsaw puzzle each piece has one
and only one proper position, which the player finds through
comparison of sizes, colors, and shapes and through a process
of elimination. The "battle of the bones," however, has the
fascination of the apparently infinite; instead of one solution,
there are many possible ones, none more inherently correct
than any other, and no piece has a fixed position. Each piece
isolated from the others is a meaningless shape, like one of
Lucretius' atoms, or like a single letter of the alphabet. Its
significance depends entirely on its position in relation to the
other pieces of the puzzle, or on its context. The game hovers
on the brink of pure randomness; it is the skill of the player
which brings a principle of order into the potential chaos. A
skilled player creates a harmony (*concinnatio*); an unskilled one

[8]From the preface to the *Cento Nuptialis* (lines 36–42), in Ausonius, *Opuscula,* ed. Sextus Prete (Leipzig, 1978).

ends up with random joinings (*iunctura*). What Ausonius does not point out, but which is obvious on a moment's contemplation of the game, is that an unskilled player may at any moment come up with arrangements indistinguishable from the harmonious arrangements of the skilled player.

Ausonius, though he is clearly fascinated with the problem, does not step over the edge into the purely random in his own poem, which is an obscene epithalamium made up entirely of lines and half-lines from the works of Vergil. This is not one of Ausonius' better received poems; the editor of Ausonius' works in the Loeb edition reacted to it with horror, declaring in his introduction that "the result is shambling and awkward as to sense, and disgraced by the crude and brutal coarseness of its closing episode. Neither the thorough knowledge of Vergil's text, nor the perverse ingenuity displayed in the compilation can redeem this literary outrage."[9]

Although the editor reacts so strongly to the obscenity of the *Cento*, there is probably more to his discomfort than puritanical shock, for, after all, Ausonius wrote other obscene poems that are not singled out for castigation.[10] Why does the cento receive the full force of his editorial wrath? It is the "thorough knowledge of Vergil's text" and the "perverse ingenuity displayed in the compilation" that most offend him—the sense of the desecration of a serious (for a Latinist, *the* serious) text. For a cento, by its very nature, works on two levels, so that the reader cannot take it as a straightforward, self-enclosed narrative. The other text, the "original" text, is always there; without it the cento would have no point. By the same token, the cento, by changing the context, and therefore the meaning of the Vergilian phrases, alters forever the reader's perception of the original Vergilian text. He cannot read the cento without recalling the original text, but after having read the cento, he cannot read the original without finding the cento intruding. This leaves the reader caught between texts, made fully aware

[9]H. G. Evelyn White, intro. to the Loeb *Ausonius: Works* (Cambridge, Mass., 1919), p. xvi–xvii.
[10]For example, epigrams 59, 78, 79, 82, 86, 87, and 93.

of the unfixed nature of language, whose elements (in this case metrical units) can be assembled and reassembled, at will or at random. But it also forces the reader to participate, for the cento's success as an amusement depends on the reader's knowledge of the Vergilian corpus and his perception of the incongruity between the language of the original text and the artificial plot contrived by Ausonius.

Sarah Spence points out that a similar expectation of audience participation operates in the paintings from the early Christian catacombs. Many of these catacombs feature figures from the Old Testament, such as Jonah, Noah, Daniel, and Susanna, figures that implicitly demand a typological reading from their audience—it is up to the audience, that is, to supply the missing information that Jonah is significant and appropriate because he is a type of the resurrected Christ. In other paintings, there are combinations of figures suggesting a significant pairing:

> For instance, . . . a scene from the *Coemeterium Maius* in which Adam and Eve are separated not only by the tree of the knowledge of good and evil but also by the healed paralytic holding up his bed, suggests that the action of the Fall has been redeemed by a miracle, that Christ has saved us from the Fall. . . . In [this instance] *the audience must supply the organizing matrix.* In and of themselves these paintings make no narrative sense: if the two stories involved in each case are not known, or if the constant that makes such a pairing is not understandable, then these scenes become meaningless.[11]

The expectation that the audience and the painter share an assumed but unstated body of knowledge that will illuminate the relationship between the figures in the catacomb paintings is similar to the assumption of Ausonius or any other cento writer that the audience and the poet share an intimate knowl-

---

[11]Spence, *Rhetorics of Reason and Desire: Vergil, Augustine, and the Troubadours* (Ithaca, N.Y., 1988), pp. 62–64, my emphasis. Spence goes on to discuss the importance of what she calls the "rhetoric of participation" in other early Christian texts, particularly in the work of Augustine.

edge of the same body of texts. Though this assumption is most blatant in a cento, it is clear from the volume of literary allusions in fourth-century poetry that the poets took for granted their audience's knowledge of classical texts.[12]

Another tendency of fourth-century poetry was toward a kind of abstract literary extremism, perhaps best represented in the work of Publilius Optatianus Porfyrius, a poet of the court of Constantine who was exiled sometime around 315 for reasons unknown.[13] While in exile, Optatian wrote a number of poems celebrating Constantine and in keeping with Constantinian propaganda. These works evidently brought about the desired result of a reconciliation with the emperor, for Optatian was recalled in 325. In his poems, words and their meanings are almost entirely subservient to his other concerns, and the poems, as poems, are practically unreadable. They are, instead, elaborate devices—metrical toys, shaped verses, palindromes, acrostics, and lines of verse that can be rearranged in a startling number of ways to generate metrically correct lines. Some of his poems are arranged so that highlighted letters in the text form complicated pictures or geometrical patterns on the page. In each case, the highlighted letters, when read in the proper sequence, form metrically correct verses of their own. Levitan, describing these peculiar poems, says,

> The poems, of course, make sense, but the impulse to verbal
> mimesis is conspicuously weak. Then we can notice Optatian's

[12]See Michael Roberts' "Paulinus Poem 11, Virgil's First Eclogue, and the Limits of *Amicitia*," *TAPhA* 115 (1985):271–282, in which he discusses Paulinus' assumption that his audience (in this case Ausonius) was familiar with classical texts and able to interpret quite subtle allusions.

[13]This poet's work recently has been analyzed elegantly by William Levitan in "Dancing at the End of the Rope: Optatian and the Field of Roman Verse," *TAPhA* 115 (1985):245–269. I merely summarize several points he makes in this article, which will reward the attention of even those readers who have no interest in Optatian. See also J. Onians, *Art and Thought in the Hellenistic Age: The Greek World View, 350–50 B.C.* (London, 1979), pp. 95–115, on epitaphs, hieroglyphs, and shaped poems; G. Polara, *Publilii Optatiani Porfyrii Carmina*, 2 vols. (Turin, 1973); and Levitan, "Plexed Artistry: Three Aratean Acrostics," *Glyph* 5 (1978):55–68.

conception of the atomistic nature of language. Not only does he
treat each line as an individual entity, or at most as half a pair,
but he doggedly analyzes the flow of speech into its elemental
constituents—the appositional phrase, the syllable, the metrical
unit, the finite parts of speech lifted from a student's grammar:
with justice, Optatian could speak of his poems as "chains." But
when language, relieved of ordinary referential or mimetic impulses, is understood to be a combination of discrete particles as
it is here, it suggests that the generation of new statements, new
linguistic possibilities, will rest solely on the mechanical combination of the same particles, subject only to the modes of
syntax and, in the case of verse, meter. A third general point
about Optatian: his poems demand just such recombination.
Lines must be read backward; metrical elements transposed;
nouns considered in grammatical cases other than those in
which they appear; individual elements of one line isolated
and . . . recombined with isolated elements of another to form
new patterns. . . . This is not to suggest that Optatian's poems
are enigmas to stymie the reader—the rules that govern recombination are plain enough . . . only that they require contemplation, as if worlds.

But what kind of worlds?[14]

What kind of worlds, indeed, were built by this exiled poet?
Liminal worlds, occupying space in two different dimensions.
In the pictorial and patterned poems, the highlighted design is
forced into the foreground and the rest of the poem fades into
the background, which has the effect of distracting the reader
and preventing him from reading the actual text (stale praises
of the emperor). The reader is pushed over the threshold of
one order of experience, reading a text, into another, seeing a
picture. Optatian's poems, written, like Ovid's *Tristia,* from a
poet in exile to an angry emperor, are, when read as conventional texts, dispirited pleas for forgiveness and repetitive
praises of Constantine. And yet, when looked at from another
perspective, they represent the transcendent freedom of the
poet, who has reconstructed his prison in the stale conven-

[14]Levitan, "Dancing at the End of the Rope," *TAPhA* (1985), pp. 249–250.

tionalities of his verse and then burst through it into a new realm, forcing the texts beyond the limits of writing to a new form of expression.

Some of Optatian's poems are pure potential. Their actuality must be generated by the reader—in other words, the poem as it appears is only one of a vast number of possible arrangements of its constituent parts. The number of arrangements depends upon each reader's ability to perceive the rules of the game. Poem 25 consists in its most basic form of four lines of dactylic hexameters, but it can be rearranged to make grammatical and metrical sense in so many ways that, as Levitan says:

> The question arises, in what does the poem consist, and where does it end? This is in the first instance a genuine historical problem since some manuscripts include only the first four lines of the poem, while all others agree on a version of seventy-two lines. . . . This historical question becomes also a question of reading. Is the poem to be understood as consisting only of the first four thematic lines, or as expanding to comprehend all their possible variations whose record would fill so many sheets of valuable parchment or so many seconds of valuable computer time? (pp. 251–252)

The text itself provides no answer; it merely sets out the raw material and the rules and leaves the reader to set his or her own limits. The cento does something similar: its rules are obvious, its possibilities endless, its effect on the reader, to judge by most critical reactions, unsettling, for it is up to him to supply the absent (con)text—the appropriate passage of Vergil, in Ausonius' or Proba's case—for every phrase. Without the reader's collaboration, the cento, as an art form, is pointless.

It is against this background that we must set the poetry of Prudentius. To understand his poetic technique, it is essential to bear in mind that he wrote at a time when the overt and radical manipulation of language was in the air. But where Ausonius in his cento and Optatian in most of his work confined themselves to metrical and visual stunts, ignoring, for the most part, the meanings of the words they played with, Prudentius worked not only on the literal, but also on the semantic level. Etymology and wordplays clearly fascinated him, as they did his contemporaries Macrobius, Servius, and even Augustine (who devotes a good deal of the *City of God* to refuting the pluralizing etymologies of Varro).[15] Much of Servius' and Macrobius' scholarship depends on etymology. Servius uses etymologies frequently in his *Aeneid* commentary. To take one example, commenting on the name Caesar, he says:

> CAESAR hic est qui dicitur Gaius Iulius Caesar. et Gaius praenomen est, Iulius ab Iulo, Caesar vel quod *caeso* matris ventre natus est vel quod avus eius in Africa manu propria occidit elephantem, qui "*caesa*" dicitur lingua Poenarum. (Servius at *Aen.* 1.262)

> Caesar is the one who is called Gaius Julius Caesar, and Gaius is his praenomen, Julius is from Iulus, and Caesar is either because he was cut (CAESO) from his mother's womb at birth, or because his grandfather killed an elephant in Africa with his own hand, and the elephant is called CAESA in the Punic language.

The etymologizing is not, as we can see, restricted to Latin: Servius is willing to derive "Caesar" from the Phoenician word for elephant, *caesa*. Similarly, in the first book of Macrobius' *Saturnalia,* much of the discussion about religion revolves around etymology, which Macrobius uses not only to explain the names of the months and the gods, but eventually to prove the Neoplatonic point that all the gods are manifestations of the one. Macrobius is particularly fond of Greek etymologies. In the same vein, Augustine and Jerome and other patristic commentators dwell at length on the meaning of biblical names.[16]

[15]See Ahl, *Metaformations,* pp. 23–24; Augustine *Civ. Dei* 4.8–13; see also A. Trapé "Augustinus et Varro," in *Atti congres. studi varroniani* 2 (1974):553–563; J. Pepin, "La théologie tripartite de Varron," *REA* 2 (1956):265–294.
[16]See Ahl, *Metaformations,* p. 62, fn. 34, for a list of works on wordplay in the Old Testament.

Prudentius works on similar principles. He puts his words
through their linguistic paces, running through all their possible meanings, making puns and anagrams, sometimes basing
entire poems on the various meanings of a single word or
name. Like Macrobius, he is fond of Greek etymologies as well
as Latin ones.[17] This fascination with language and with the
transformation of meaning brought about by rearrangement
of the same set of letters reflects Prudentius' preoccupation
with transformations and threshholds on all levels. His poems
are hard to follow because they tend to progress by a series of
dislocations, jumps that move the characters and the reader
from one order of experience to another, often without any
obvious reason.[18] Sometimes the point of transition between
states is clear, as in *Peristephanon* 14, in which the young virgin
Agnes is beheaded. This violent death enables her soul to leap
from earth to heaven, where it is treated to a supernatural
vision of the transitory nature of the material world. At other
times Prudentius' characters undergo more subtle transformations. Cassian, for example, the stern schoolmaster and
martyr of *Peristephanon* 9, is stabbed to death by the pens of his
vengeful pupils and thus not only achieves martyrdom but
also epitomizes the fate of all biographical subjects, who turn
from living flesh into dead text.

[17]John Francis Petrucione, "Prudentius' Use of Martyrological Topoi in
Peristephanon," diss., University of Michigan, 1985, pp. 40–41, draws attention to Prudentius' fondness for using bilingual wordplays on the meaning of
his saints' Greek names. It is tempting to conclude that Prudentius gave his
poems Greek titles to draw attention to this aspect of his verse, but see
M. Brozek, "De librorum Prudentii inscriptionibus graecis," *Eos* 71 (1983):
191–197, who argues that only *Hamartagenia, Apotheosis,* and *Psychomachia*
are Prudentius' own titles. If Brozek is correct, we must extend belated
congratulations to the compiler who gave the *Peristephanon* its title, for as I
argue in Chapter 6, the image of the crown is essential to the book.

[18]Cf. what Frederick Ahl says about Statius' poetry: "What Statius' letter to
Marcellus shows us, above all else, is that one must read between the lines.
The text makes sense only when the missing steps in the logical progression
of thought are supplied by the reader. There is a curious and calculated
discontinuity in his manner which forces the reader into a kind of intellectual
dialogue with him": Ahl, "The Rider and the Horse: Politics and Power in
Roman Poetry from Horace to Statius," *ANRW* 2, no. 1 (1984):40–110.

Sometimes it is even the poet himself who undergoes some sort of transformation. Like Alfred Hitchcock in his films, Prudentius is frequently a character in his own poems, and he often ends them with a prayer for his own soul. He follows this pattern in one of his more daunting theological treatises, the *Hamartigenia,* a poem nearly three thousand lines long which opens with the familiar Roman theme of fratricide (though Cain and Abel have replaced Romulus and Remus as the archetypal feuding brothers) and goes on to consider the evils of dualism and the corruption of the material world through human sin. It ends with a prayer, the last lines of which have vexed editors, for Prudentius seems to be advocating a doctrine of Purgatory that is anachronistic, and his language, especially in the final line, is peculiar.[19] The prayer ends with these lines:

> Esto, cavernoso, quia sic pro labe necesse est
> corporea, tristis me sorbeat ignis Averno;
> saltem mitificos incendia lenta vapores
> exhalent, aestuque calor languente tepescat;
> lux inmensa alios et tempora vincta coronis
> glorificent, me poena levis clementer adurat.
> (Ham. 961–966)

So be it. Let me sink into the sad flames of cavernous Avernus. This is necessary: material corruption demands it. But I hope at least that the slow burning fires will breathe forth mild steam, and that their heat becomes impotent and loses its blazing intensity. Others may find glory in crowns that bind their temples, and in limitless light—as for me, may a light punishment burn me leniently.

Here Prudentius acknowledges that he will have to be punished for *labe . . . corporea,* which might be translated as either "original sin" or "material corruption." He hopes the fires will be slow and the heat only lukewarm, and finally he contrasts

[19]See Roberto Palla's discussion of the final prayer in the *Hamartigenia* in his edition of the poem (Pisa, 1981), pp. 310–312.

the fate of some unspecified others (*alios*) who will have their temples bound with crowns, with his own, asking that his own punishment be light (*levis*) and burn him leniently (*clementer*). This is an odd, even an awkward conclusion to the poem. It is strange to find Prudentius, who frequently uses the ancient topos of the poet's crown and who calls his own poems garlands or crowns, ending a poem by ceding to others his claims to a crown, and stranger still is the concept of a light punishment that would burn leniently. Two oxymorons in a row (*poena levis* and *clementer adurat*) call special attention to the final phrase.

At this point, an awareness of the possibility of punning wordplay can help us. The adverb *clementer,* the penultimate word in the poem, suggests the poet's own name, Aurelius Prudentius Clemens. The humility of Prudentius' prayer is somewhat compromised by this play on his own name in the important last line of the poem. This slight incongruity between Prudentius' professed abnegation of self and his insistence on calling attention to himself through the play on his own name may, indeed, be the key to the transformation that occurs in the final line of the poem. *Clementer,* almost but not quite the same as the poet's own name, taken in conjunction with the *me* earlier in the same line, is both a failed signature (it suggests the poet's name, but is not his name) and a signal to the reader to examine the verse more carefully. And if we decide to take up the challenge and play with the verse, we discover that the words following the *me* can be resolved into an anagram, if we remember that *u* and *v* are treated as one letter in Latin. POENA LEVIS CLEMENTER ADVRAT becomes AVRELIO PRVDENTE SE CLAMANTE: "Aurelius the Prudent proclaiming himself." Thus the entire last line, when the anagram is set forth, reads: *glorificent me: Aurelio Prudente se clamante,* "let them glorify me: Aurelius the Prudent proclaiming himself."

The exigencies of the anagram go a long way toward explaining the awkwardness of the last line. One of the interesting features of the anagram, apart from its rather impressive length, is that the clue that tips the reader off that there is some sort of play on the poet's name is itself a trick, for when the anagram is unscrambled, the Clemente, which one would expect to find, is not there. Instead, there is the participle *clamante.* Similarly, the *me,* which also draws attention to the identity of the poet, and which in the original line belongs grammatically to the last part of the sentence (which contains the anagram), must change its affiliation when the sentence is unscrambled to become the object of *glorificent.* It is not part of the anagram, although it points to it. *Me* and *clementer* are the threshold words that allow us to make the transition from the original verse to the anagram: they can take us up to the point of transition, but when we cross over into the new dimension, they disappear.

I have chosen the anagram as an example of Prudentius' poetic method because it shows how much of Prudentius we lose if we read him as a "straightforward" narrator. Not all of Prudentius' poetry relies on anagrams and wordplays, but the anagram does demonstrate that, like Ausonius or Optatian, he relies on us, his readers, to take the extra steps, to supply the information, to make the final equation, which he will not or cannot make for us. This reliance on the reader makes his poetry extremely difficult to approach: classicists are not trained to read texts as cryptograms. Yet once we learn to recognize the clues the poet so carefully provides, we can begin to travel with some confidence through the strange new world of his poetry.

In the next chapter, I turn to Prudentius' *Psychomachia,* his epic of the inner space of the soul, and examine his development of the conflict between Concord and Discord which concludes the battle between the Virtues and the Vices. I begin by looking at one of the sources for Prudentius' climactic battle scene: the death of Rufinus as described by Prudentius' contemporary Claudian in his *In Rufinum.*

3

Words at War

Prudentius' younger contemporary Claudian appears superficially to have been everything Prudentius was not. They were from different parts of the empire—Prudentius from Spain, Claudian from Alexandria. Prudentius was a Latin speaker from a province with a proud literary heritage; Claudian was not a native Latin speaker and composed a number of poems in Greek. Prudentius wrote poetry on Christian subjects, Claudian on traditional pagan themes, such as his unfinished short epic, *De raptu Proserpinae*. Claudian's poetry relies heavily on the traditional apparatus of mythology, while Prudentius (not surprisingly for a poet who writes on Christian themes) eliminated the pagan gods as active participants in the action of his poems. But perhaps the greatest difference is that Claudian was an overtly political poet—much of his poetry was based on contemporary political events—while Prudentius concentrated on metaphysical and theological subjects that seem to have little bearing on the politics of his day.

And yet despite the apparently radical differences between the two men, the relationship between them deserves, as Alan Cameron has suggested, closer study.[1] Not only is there ample evidence of allusions to Claudian in Prudentius' poetry (and, as Cameron suggests, evidence of borrowings from Pruden-

[1]Alan Cameron, *Claudian: Poetry and Propaganda at the Court of Honorius* (Oxford, 1970), app. B.

tius in Claudian's), but it can be shown that the two men shared basic thematic preoccupations. Although Prudentius maps the metaphysical realm and Claudian the historical and political, there is a strange congruence in their poetic techniques and in the unstable and often frightening worlds they describe. This similarity goes beyond shared themes and imagery to the way both poets manipulate the classical poetic tradition and to their use of language. In this chapter I begin with a look at how Claudian treats a traditional topos—the *sparagmos*, or dismemberment—and uses it as an emblem for civil strife. I then examine Prudentius' use of the same motif and his development of ideas present in the Claudian passage in the climactic scene of his *Psychomachia*. This scene, the final battle of the war between the personified Virtues and Vices, contains many of the same thematic preoccupations with *discordia* and with thresholds and boundary violations as the *Peristephanon* poems discussed in the next chapters. We also find in both works a persistent tension between imagery of binding and weaving on the one hand and dismemberment and dissolution on the other. An elucidation of Prudentius' sources and his manipulation of language in this scene are a useful introduction to the more complicated and subtle poems of the *Peristephanon*. I focus here on Concord and Discord in the *Psychomachia*, figures with their own genealogy in epic poetry, and conclude by considering the philosophic and political implications of Prudentius' use of the duel between these two figures to end the battle within the soul which forms the subject of the poem.

The Death of Rufinus

In Rufinum is Claudian's often surrealistic caricature of the career of Rufinus, the man the Western imperial court loved to hate.[2] Rufinus was the praetorian prefect of the Eastern

[2]Cameron, *Claudian*, pp. 63–92, discusses Rufinus' career and some of the political reasons for Claudian's savage treatment of him in the poem. For

empire who dominated the ineffectual young emperor Arcadius. The second book of the poem, written not long after Rufinus' dramatic death in 395, has as its climax Rufinus' gruesome assassination at the hands of the army, which took place before the eyes of Arcadius himself. Rufinus is literally torn to pieces by a mob of furious soldiers; in Claudian's version of the story, when the people of Constantinople hear the news, they pour out of the city gates to join in the dismemberment.[3]

Claudian surrounds his account of Rufinus' death with imagery that is both haunting and significant. The actual dismemberment, as we shall see, conjures up predictable allusions to Pentheus (dismembered by a band of Bacchants led by his own mother) and the unfortunate hunter Actaeon (ripped to pieces by his own dogs). Before the actual death, however, Claudian sets the stage for it in a simile comparing Rufinus to a beast doomed to die in the arena:

> ut fera, quae nuper montes amisit avitos
> altorumque exul nemorum damnatur harenae
> muneribus, commota ruit; vir murmure contra
> hortatur nixusque genu venabula tendit;
> illa pavet strepitus cuneosque erecta theatri
> respicit et tanti miratur sibila vulgi.
>
> <div align="right">(<i>In Ruf.</i> 2.396–399)</div>

Like a beast who has just been exiled from the mountains where her fathers roamed, banished from the high forests, she is doomed to the games in the arena. She runs in terror; encouraged by the noise, the man kneels to set his net. She is afraid, and standing erect, she looks back at the uproar in the stands of the theater and marvels at the hissing of the huge mob.

This simile does not work, as one might expect it to, as another demonstration of Rufinus' bestiality. Instead, the poet rather

---

more about Rufinus, see also the introduction to Harry Levy's edition of *In Rufinum* (New York, 1935).

[3]Cameron, *Claudian,* pp. 63–66, 90–92.

subtly emphasizes the human characteristics of the doomed animal in the arena. Once free to wander in the mountains and woods, she is now in exile from her native land and condemned to take part in the gladiatorial games which, as the Roman poets never tired of pointing out, were originally a form of human sacrifice. The beast, through her role in the *muneribus,* acquires the characteristics of a human being: she is endowed with ancestors and a homeland (*avitos montes*); she suffers from emotion (*commota, pavet*); finally, when she hears the crowd and sees the theater, she stands erect (*erecta*) and marvels (*respicit, miratur*) at the animal-like hissings of the mob. The last detail alludes to a philosophic commonplace, that humans alone of all the animals stand erect and look at the heavens and so are inspired to reason. The beast of the simile is thus, at the moment of death, made human by the atrocity she is about to suffer. In the same way, Rufinus, though an entirely unsympathetic and grotesque character throughout the poem, becomes almost human in light of the gruesome death he is about to suffer.

The image suggests another curious reversal of roles as well. Claudian, a pagan poet with little sympathy for Christian conservatism, has nevertheless appropriated one of the archetypal images of Christian martyrdom: death in the arena.[4]

---

[4]Cf. Tertullian *De spectaculis* 29, a passage that anticipates the psychic battles of the *Psychomachia:*

> haec voluptates, haec spectacula Christianorum sancta perpetua gratuita; in his tibi circenses ludos interpretare, cursus saeculi intuere, tempora labentia, spatia peracta dinumera, metas consummationis exspecta, societates ecclesiarum defende, ad signum dei suscitare, ad tubam angeli erigere, ad martyrum palmas gloriare. . . . Vis et pugilatus et luctatus? praesto sunt, non parva et multa. Aspice impudicitiam deiectam a castitate, perfidiam caesam a fide, saevitiam a misericordia contusam, petulantium a modestia adumbratum, et tales sunt apud nos agones, in quibus ipsi coronamur.

> These are the pleasures and the spectacles of the Christians: holy, eternal, and free of charge. In these recognize your circus games; watch the race of time and the gliding seasons; count the laps that have been driven; wait for the finish of the final testing; defend the teams of the churches; jump up when you see the banner of god; stand up straight when you hear the angel's horn; rejoice in the victories of the martyrs. . . . You want boxing and wrestling matches? Here they are, and there are many and important ones. Look

The image of the martyr as the athlete of God, winning victory
through death in combat, reaches back to the earliest days of
the church. But whereas the Christians went unarmed against
the wild beasts of the arena, Claudian shows us the more sport-
ing form of gladiatorial combat, with an armed man facing a
beast—in this case, a curiously human, defenseless beast. This
inversion of the Christian trope is, perhaps, ironic—Claudian
may have particularly enjoyed casting Rufinus in the role of
"martyred" beast, for he was known for his aggressive persecution of pagans and heretics and for his particular devotion to
the cult of the martyrs. He even had a martyrium built at his
home in Chalcedon which contained the relics of Saints Peter
and Paul (acquired in Rome in 389) and imported a community of monks from Egypt to conduct services.[5]

This reversal of roles extends, as we shall see, beyond the
simile to the murder of Rufinus, which one would expect,
from the tone of the poem up to this point, to result in the
purging of evil from the body politic. Claudian has certainly
made no bones about casting Rufinus as the embodiment of
evil, but his death does not, in fact, perform this cleansing
function. Instead of ending the savagery Rufinus epitomizes,
his death, ironically, spreads murderous violence throughout
the army and the civilian population. Claudian prefigures the
dehumanizing effect of violence on those who commit it in this
striking passage, which has the ring of science fiction in its
eerie metamorphosis:

> huc ultrix acies ornatu lucida Martis
> explicuit cuneos. pedites in parte sinistra
> consistunt. equites illinc poscentia cursum
> ora reluctantur pressis sedere lupatis;
> hinc alii saevum cristato vertice nutant

---

at shamelessness thrown to the ground by chastity; faithlessness by faith;
cruelty stunned by mercy; wantonness overshadowed by modesty. Such are
the contests among us, in which we ourselves win crowns.

[5]John Matthews, *Western Aristocracies and the Imperial Court:* A.D. *364–425*
(Oxford, 1975), pp. 134–136.

et tremulos umeris gaudent vibrare colores.
quos operit formatque chalybs; coniuncta per artem
flexilis inductis animatur lamina membris
horribiles visu; credas simulacra moveri
ferrea cognatoque viros spirare metallo.

(In Ruf. 2.351–360)

Now the avenging army, glittering in the spoils of war, deployed its ranks. Foot soldiers stand together on the left; near them horsemen saw at the reins, fighting to restrain their beasts, who yearn to gallop. Over here other men savagely shake their crested heads, making the trembling colors dance along their armored shoulders. Hard iron shrouds and shapes them: artfully joined, link by link, the supple steel breathes life from the flesh inside. It's a horrible sight—you'd think they were moving metal statues, or that men in metal casings could breathe.

The crowd in the arena simile, massed in ranks, *cuneos,* like the soldiers in this passage, become like wild beasts in their anticipation of the bloody games about to take place. The soldiers here, waiting to take part in the murder of Rufinus, undergo a more sinister transformation. In the lines that describe the soldiers and their armor (357–360), the distinction between the animate and the inanimate begins to blur: the armor is alive and seems to draw energy from the men hidden inside it. Claudian emphasizes this strange symbiosis with an anagrammatic wordplay: there is ANIMA, spirit or breath, in the LAMINA, the armor that wraps itself around the limbs of the soldiers; moreover, when read backwards, the word for armor reveals what it is becoming: ANIMAL. This metamorphosis moves both ways, for as the lifeless metal becomes a living thing, the living soldiers become moving statues. These soldiers, hovering between the animate and the inanimate, form a fitting escort for Rufinus as he sets off to his death, for they are *liminal* figures and Rufinus, too, though unwittingly, is poised on the threshold between life and death.

In the actual death scene, we find once more the implication that violence transforms the aggressor into something less than human:

hi vultus avidos et adhuc spirantia vellunt
lumina, truncatos alii rapuere lacertos.
amputat ille pedes, umerum quatit ille solutis
nexibus; hic fracti reserat curvamina dorsi;
hic iecur, hic cordis fibras, hic pandit anhelas
pulmonis latebras. spatium non invenit ira
nec locus est odiis. consumpto funere vix tum
deseritur sparsumque perit per tela cadaver.
sic mons Aonius rubuit, cum Penthea ferrent
Maenades aut subito mutatum Actaeona cornu
traderet insanis Latonia visa Molossis.

(*In Ruf.* 2.410–420)

Some tear at his greedy face and his eyes, still flashing with life; others tear his arms out by the roots and carry them off. One man cuts off a foot, another shakes a shoulder free from its disintegrating joints. One unhinges the curved ribs from his broken spine; one lays bare his liver; someone else explores the gasping caverns of his lungs. Rage can find no space, there is no room for hatred. But even when his death was more than certain, they could hardly leave him, and so they carried his ruined body home on their spears. It was like this when the Aonian mountain turned red with blood when the Maenads slaughtered Pentheus, and when Diana, suddenly discovered, betrayed Actaeon—now a stag, not a man—to his Molossian hounds.

As the attackers dismember Rufinus' body, the crowd becomes fragmented, losing its unanimity and becoming not a group but a collection of individuals, each bent on his own gory task, as *hi . . . alii* gives way in the text to *ille . . . ille . . . hic . . . hic . . . hic*, each man tearing his own piece from the battered body. The men are compared to the Bacchae, who roam the mountains, free of the bonds that hold society together, and to the hounds of Actaeon, who turn on their no longer human master.

Claudian has led us through a series of reversals: Rufinus, through the beast simile, loses his savagery and becomes, for a moment, a human victim, while the soldiers and the people of Constantinople are transformed from Rufinus' long-suffering victims to savage predators. Claudian has used similes, wordplay, and striking imagery to reiterate a theme that the Roman poets, steeped in Rome's bitter heritage of civil strife, return to again and again: that violence is infectious and that you can defeat an enemy only by taking his place—by becoming, that is, what you have fought against. It is this stark vision that prevents *In Rufinum* from falling into the category of sheer personal abuse, for Claudian's concern is more than the simple condemnation of a fallen political enemy. He analyzes the spread of violence, from the top down, through society as a whole.

The Battlefield of Semantics

This concern with the spread of violence and with the uncertain boundaries between friend and foe, victim and victor, is shared by Prudentius and expressed most clearly and dramatically in the *Psychomachia,* his allegorical epic of the inner space of the soul.[6] In a sense, the *Psychomachia* proceeds logically from the groundwork established by Claudian. In the dismemberment scene quoted above, Claudian moves his characters out of the world of the city for the climactic scene of dismemberment. As Rufinus, the soldiers, and finally the citizens of Constantinople leave the civic space enclosed by the city walls, Claudian marks this transition by similes that place the characters in the world of myth. Rufinus' death is described in paradigmatic, mythic terms—he is Pentheus and

---

[6]For other interpretations of the *Psychomachia,* see Macklin Smith, *Prudentius' "Psychomachia": A Reexamination* (Princeton, N.J., 1976); S. Georgia Nugent, *Allegory and Poetics: The Structure and Imagery of Prudentius' "Psychomachia"* (Frankfurt, 1974); Christian Gnilka, *Studien zur "Psychomachie" des Prudentius* (Wiesbaden, 1963); Klaus Thraede, *Studien zu Sprache und Stil des Prudentius* (Gottingen, 1965); C. S. Lewis, *The Allegory of Love,* rev. ed. (Oxford, 1963); Kenneth R. Haworth, *Deified Virtues, Demonic Vices, and Descriptive Allegory in Prudentius' "Psychomachia"* (Amsterdam, 1980); E. Rapisarda, *Psychomachia: testo con introduzione e traduzione* (Catania, 1962); Reinhart Herzog, *Die allegorische Dichtkunst des Prudentius, Zetemata* vol. 42 (Munich, 1966). For a general discussion of theories of allegory in the classical and late antique periods, see Robert Lamberton, *Homer the Theologian: Neoplatonist Allegorical Reading and the Growth of the Epic Tradition* (Berkeley, Calif., 1986).

Actaeon—rather than as a historic incident. And as Rufinus takes on mythic dimensions at the end of the poem, the danger he represents is shown to be something more than the appalling behavior of a single human being. His anger and hatred infect the mob of citizens and soldiers to such an extent that they cannot be contained even after Rufinus is completely disintegrated (*spatium non invenit ira nec locus est odiis*, lines 416–417).

In the *Psychomachia*, Prudentius shows us anger and hatred raging on in battle although his poem takes place in no definable time or space. The locus is not history or even myth, but the timeless world of the psyche, and as the setting is eliminated, so, in a way, are the characters. Instead of using political figures, as Claudian does, or characters from myth, as was the usual epic practice, Prudentius takes the radical step of peopling the blank world of his poem with abstractions—mere words.[7] Prudentius, of course, was not the first writer to introduce personified abstractions as characters in his work. The technique goes back at least as far as the figures on the shield of Achilles in *Iliad* 18, in which Strife, Uproar, and Fate are shown participating in a battle scene. More elaborately, Xenophon shows Heracles forced to choose between Pleasure and Virtue, two abstractions personified as women,[8] and Euripides has Lyssa, the personification of madness, appear as a character in his *Heracles Mainomenos*. Vergil, too, uses personified abstractions in the *Aeneid*, as in this passage describing the gates of Hell:

> vestibulum ante ipsum primusque in faucibus Orci
> Luctus et ultrices posuere cubilia Curae,
> pallantesque habitant Morbi tristisque Senectus,

---

[7]Haworth, *Deified Virtues*, demonstrates that a number of the Virtues mentioned in the *Psychomachia* were personified forces actually worshipped in the ancient world, a point worth emphasizing. The cult of personified virtues may well have influenced Prudentius' descriptions of the Virtues' appearance and costumes, but my emphasis here is on Prudentius' fascination with the nature of language and the idea of verbal abstractions.

[8]*Iliad* 18.530ff.; Xenophon *Memorabilia* 2.1.

et metus et malesuada Fames ac turpis Egestas,
terribilis visu formae, Letumque Labosque,
tum consanguineus Letis Sopor et mala mentis
Gaudia, mortiferumque adversum in limine Bellum,
ferreique Eumenidum thalami et Discordia demens
vipereumque crinem vittis innexa cruentis.

(*Aen.* 6.273–281)

Before the very entrance, just inside the jaws of Orcus, Grief
and the vengeful Cares have set their couches. There live the
pale and trembling Diseases and sad Old Age, Fear and evil-
counseling Hunger, and squalid Poverty—shapes horrible to
see. And Death is there, and Toil; Death's brother Sleep and the
evil Pleasures of the mind. Facing these on the threshold are
deadly War, the iron chambers of the Furies, and mad Discord,
her hair bound with sacred ribbons stained with blood.

Vergil, however, seldom shows us his abstractions interacting
with his other characters. They are there to form allegorical set
pieces, and they remain outside the main action of the epic.
This is not true in the strange and chaotic world of Statius'
Thebaid, in which gods, humans, and personified abstractions
mix indiscriminately, and any action carried out at one level of
the narrative reverberates through the whole. Prudentius, in
the *Psychomachia,* carries Statius' technique to its logical extreme—he eliminates the human characters entirely, except
for occasional Old Testament figures in the background. (One
could argue that he sees these as allegorical as well—figural
types who foreshadow New Testament personages and symbolize the state of the individual soul.) Only the abstractions
remain.[9]

In Prudentius' poem, the words themselves do battle, carrying out their struggle on the field of semantics. As the personified abstractions move through their series of combats, it
becomes evident that puns, etymological wordplays, allusions

[9]There are hints of this sort of allegorical treatment of personified abstractions in other early Christian sources—for example, the Tertullian passage
cited above in this chapter and Methodius' *Symp.* 8.172, in which the world
appears as a stage and mankind is faced with demonic adversaries.

to classical and biblical texts, and similes are more than elaborate ornaments decorating the surface of the text. Rather, they control the action and shape of the poem. The function of Prudentius' allegory is not simply to tell a story—the *Psychomachia* has very little plot, and what there is is entirely predictable—but also to force the reader to become a player in Prudentius' poetic game. Like the player of the *ostomachia*, the reader of the *Psychomachia* is free to manipulate the poetic "bones" into whatever semblance of reality he chooses (with helpful hints provided by the poet).

In the *Psychomachia* Prudentius appears to have created a new genre of poetry, and in so doing, he has laid his poetic cards on the table. His choice of the sustained personification allegory directs the reader's attenton to his treatment of characters not as people or as symbols whose meaning is always fixed, but as signs whose meaning is variable and inconstant. The paradox of Prudentius' technique is that by creating iconographically clear allegorical figures out of words, and giving them the ability to act, he endows his abstractions with all the inconsistencies and ambiguities of human characters.

Concordia and Discordia

The *Psychomachia*, in a sense, has a false ending. The poem consists of seven battles, each between one or more of the Virtues, who are professed Christians, and the Vices, who, in addition to being vicious, are pagans as well. Like the simile in Claudian's *In Rufinum* which we examined above, the battles here suggest the arena rather than the battlefield as their setting. In most cases, the fighting in the poem is done in single combat. But despite the gladiatorial atmosphere, the Virtues in the poem are by no means martyrs. They do not submit to death and claim it as a form of victory, but rather they participate in combat ferociously and inflict gruesome wounds and hideous deaths upon their enemies. A number of critics have noticed the paradox of this unchristian bloodthirstiness in the Virtues, but they generally have ascribed it to

Prudentius' and his era's lack of good taste or to his Spanish blood.[10] In the analysis of the battle between Concordia and Discordia which follows I suggest an alternative explanation for the Virtues' puzzling behavior, for the outcome of their combat, which seems to end forever the battle in the soul, is not as decisive a victory for the Virtues as it appears to be.

After the Virtues seem to have defeated their enemies conclusively in six major battles, Concordia appears on the scene, leading the victorious army into the walls of their camp. The army, however, has been infiltrated: Concordia's opposite, Discordia, has thrown off the whip and torn robe that emblematize her disruptive power and assumed the dress, the pacific olive wreath, and the joyful expression of the Virtues. Thus disguised, she gets close enough to Concordia to attack her with a concealed weapon. She is unable to kill the Virtue, but she does manage to inflict a flesh wound, the only casualty the Virtues suffer in the war.

The infuriated Virtues instantly surround Discordia and demand to know her name, her allegiance, and who sent her. She replies with a disjointed but disdainful speech, announcing that she is Discord, also known as Heresy, and that the god she worships is ever changing and inconstant. Her short speech so angers and alarms Fides that she transfixes Discordia's tongue with a javelin (one of several instances of mutilated tongues in Prudentius' poetry).[11] Once Discordia's tongue has been pinned, the rest of the Virtues descend upon her and tear her limb from limb, just as the vengeful soldiers tore apart the wretched Rufinus. The remains of her dismem-

[10]For example, Lavarenne in his introduction to Prudentius' collected works says (my translation from the French): "Unfortunately, there are also gross defects in his work which seem to stem both from the times in which he lived and from his Spanish origin" (p. xii); and, "he is notable, finally, for a predilection for horrible details, a predilection which Prudentius shares with his compatriots, Seneca and Lucan" (p. xiii). Prudentius, *Oeuvres* vol. 1, ed. Maurice Lavarenne (Paris, 1955).

[11]See my discussion in Chapter 5 of Cyprian's tongue in *Peristephanon* 13 and compare *Peristephanon* 10.895–925, in which the martyr Romanus loses his tongue but is miraculously able to deliver a *long* and impassioned speech without it.

bered body are hurled to the beasts of the earth, sea, and sky. This scene recalls not only the death of Rufinus but also the brutal dismemberment of the classical hero Hippolytus, as we shall see in the next chapter.

Throughout the episode, Prudentius puts a particular emphasis on thresholds, stressing the liminality of the scene. When Discordia makes her appearance, for example, the Virtues are just about to cross the double-doored entrance to their camp. Prudentius packs his verses with words that mean door, threshold, entrance, hinge, and so on:

> ventum erat ad fauces portae castrensis, ubi artum
> liminis introitum bifori dant cardine claustra.
> nascitur hic inopina Mali lacrimabilis astu
> tempestas, placidae turbatrix invida Pacis
> quae tantum subita vexaret clade triumphum.
>
> (*Ps.* 665–669)

They had come to the mouth of the camp gate, where the bolts hung on the hinge of the double doors opened a narrow entry to the threshold. Here a sudden cyclone springs up: born of the cunning of that lamentable Evil, the jealous one who shatters placid Peace, it would whirl the great triumph into sudden slaughter.

The description of the entrance is unusually elaborate; the threshold, with its well-defended gates, marks the boundary between the Virtues' camp and the battlefield. Discordia, by her very nature, is best suited to functioning in just such an ambiguous area, for it is characteristic of her to be neither one thing nor another. She is a master of disguise, and it is her ability to be indistinguishable from the Virtues that makes her the most dangerous of all the Vices. Prudentius' description of her disguise, particularly by his allusion to classical texts, reinforces this aspect of her nature:

> nam pulsa Culparum acie Discordia nostros
> intrarat cuneos sociam mentita figuram,

scissa procul palla structum et serpente flagellum
multiplici media camporum in strage iacebant.
ipsa redimitos olea frondente capillos
ostentans festis respondet laeta choraeis.

                                        (*Ps.* 683–688)

For when the army of the Faults had been beaten back, Discordia entered our ranks as an ally, her shape transformed. Her torn robe and whip of twisted snakes were lying far away at the center of the battlefield's web of slaughter. Holding high her head, she happily joins the victory song.

Discordia's snaky whip is an obvious allusion to the Furies; interestingly enough, the disguise she wears links her to the Furies as much as her normal costume does. Prudentius has modeled his scene on *Aeneid* 7, in which the Fury Allecto appears in disguise to incite Turnus to war:

Allecto torvam faciem et furalia membra
exuit in vultus sese transformat anilis
et frontam obscenam rugis arat, induit albos
cum vitta crinis, tum ramum innectit olivae.
                                        (*Aen.* 7.415–418)

Allecto shed her twisted frown and her Fury's form and changed herself into the shape of an old woman, tracing furrows on her obscene brow. She put on white hair and a sacred headband woven with an olive branch.

In this passage Allecto appears to the sleeping Turnus disguised as Calybe ("Veiled One"), a priestess of Juno. Like Discordia, she transforms her features and wears a wreath of deceptively peaceful olive in her snowy hair. Her mission is to bring Turnus and the Latins to war with the Trojans by driving Turnus mad with jealousy and battle lust; she is thus the immediate catalyst for the war that breaks out between the two races who would one day found Rome. In a similar scene from the *Thebaid*, the ghost of Oedipus' father Laius appears to his grandson Eteocles; his purpose, like Allecto's, is to provide the immediate impulse for war, this time between the feuding sons of Oedipus, Eteocles and his twin brother Polyneices. Laius' ghost, like Allecto and Discordia, assumes a false appearance for his mission: he puts on the form of Tiresias, the blind seer, and his hair, too, is bound with a deceptive olive wreath.[12] By adopting this topos, Prudentius makes ambiguity and false appearance as much a part of Discordia's nature as strife and violence. Discordia's ability to assimilate herself to her opponents is remarkable, and Prudentius subtly emphasizes this by his verse. As soon as the olive wreath is twined into the Vice's now neatly bound hair, there is a perfect golden line (a five-word hexameter line with a symmetrical arrangement of nouns and adjectives around a central verb). As Discordia's normal attributes are cloaked by her peaceful disguise, the verse achieves apparent harmony in a line that shows her singing in concert with the army of Virtues: *ostentans festis respondet laeta choreis.*

Concordia, who bears the brunt of Discordia's sneak attack, is also distinguished by a significant costume. She is clad in a remarkable suit of bristling armor, which Prudentius describes in verses that themselves bristle with densely packed *c, t, x,* and *s* sounds:

> inter confertos cuneos Concordia forte
> dum stipata pedem iam tutis moenibus infert,
> excipit occultum Vitii latitantis ab ictu
> mucronem laevo in latere, squalentia quamvis
> texta catenato ferri subtegmine corpus
> ambirent sutis et acumen vulneris hamis
> respuerent, rigidis nec fila tenacia nodis

[12]Statius *Theb.* 2.94–100: "tunc senior quae iussus agit, neu falsa videri / noctis imago queat, longaevi vatis opacos / Tiresiae vultus vocemque et vellera nota / induitur. mansere comae compexaque mento / canities pallorque suus, sed falsa cucurrit / infula per crines, glaucaeque innexus olivae / vittarum provenit honos" (Then the old man does what he is ordered, and lest he should seem to be a false image of the night, he puts on the shadowy features, the voice, and the familiar fillets of the long-lived seer Tiresias. His hair, the white beard combed over his chin, and his own pallor remained, but a false headband ran through his hair and an ornament woven of grey-green olive was clearly visible.)

impactum sinerent penetrare in viscera telum.
rara tamen chalybem tenui transmittere puncto
commissura dedit, qua sese extrema politae
squama ligat tunicae, sinus et sibi conserit oras.

(Ps. 670–680)

Concordia by chance was coming through the congregated companies of men, surrounded by a crowd, ready to set foot at last inside the safety of the walls. Suddenly her left side felt a hidden blade, the blow of the lurking Vice, though a scaly fabric woven from chains of steel wound about her body, repelling wounding weapons with woven hooks, and the tenacious threads, tied in rigid knots, would not allow a weapon's thrust to penetrate her heart. But just on the edge where the outer links of the bright tunic joined with the breastpiece, a fine blade slipped through the boundary between the pieces.

Concordia is characterized by language and imagery that strongly suggest restraint and enclosure—so strongly, indeed, that one might say she is caricatured rather than characterized. She appears surrounded by a crowd of massed soldiers (*confertos cuneos*), and her movement is toward the inside of the massively fortified camp. Not only do her circumstances and her movements suggest enclosure, but the description of her armor abounds with images of binding and restraint. The armor is woven from chain mail (*squalentia . . . texta catenato ferri*); its stiff threads are tied together in rigid knots (*rigidis . . . fila tenacia nodis*). The only chink in her armor is, significantly, at the boundary between two of its parts, the liminal area that belongs by rights to Discordia, whose own disintegrating dress is the exact opposite of Concordia's tightly woven chain mail.

Discordia Dismembered

Discordia, as we have seen, represents not only physical disintegration and dismemberment, but also disguise and deceit. Her speech after her capture reveals her essential person-

ality and raises serious questions about the nature of language
in the poem:

> circumstat propere strictis mucronibus omnis
> Virtutum legio exquirens fervente tumultu
> et genus et nomen, patriam sectamque, deumque
> quem colat et missu cuiatis venerit. illa
> exsanguis turbante metu: "Discordia dicor,
> cognomento Heresis; Deus est mihi discolor," inquit,
> "nunc minor aut maior, modo duplex et modo simplex,
> cum placet, aerius et de phantasmate visus,
> aut innata anima est quotiens volo ludere numen;
> praeceptor Belia mihi, domus et plaga mundus.
>
> (Ps. 705–714)

Instantly the whole army of Virtues surrounds her, swords
drawn, demanding through the seething confusion her family,
her name, her country, and her sect, which God she worshipped,
and who had sent her. White with whirling fear, she says: "I am
called Discord. My other name is Heresy. My God is variable—
sometimes small, sometimes huge; sometimes two, sometimes
one. When I wish, he seems like an airy phantom; or when I
want to play tricks with divine power, he is the inborn soul. Belial
is my teacher, the world is my territory and my home."

Despite her fear, Discordia is able to identify herself in a series
of soundplays on her name, linking the concept of *discordia*
with language and the shifting world of false appearances.
The punning echoes of her own name in the series *Discordia
dicor . . . Deus est mihi discolor* suggest, through the repetition of
rhyming syllables, that the act of speech itself (*dicor*) is a form
of *discordia*—the unreliable sounds that shift their meaning
according to context in a Lucretian manner seem to demonstrate the impossibility of finding stable signs to represent true
meanings. The use of the adjective *discolor*, "of variable color,"
appears motivated by its sound, allowing Prudentius, through
the similarity of the words, to establish a connection with the
world of shifting appearances on etymological grounds. *Dis-*

color is a relatively unusual adjective; perhaps the best known use of it is in *Aeneid* 6, in which it describes the strange appearance of the golden bough, the mysterious token that allows Aeneas to make the transition from the world of the living to the world below.[13] If this echo is deliberate, it reminds us once again that Discordia is constantly associated with liminal areas.

Discordia calls attention to her own facility with wordplay when she boasts of her different definitions of God—she calls this playing (*ludere*) with his divinity (*numen*). In fact, she has just finished reeling off a series of plays on her own *nomen*. By including *deus* in the series of words playing off the sounds of *discordia*, she has attempted to confine God, the master binder himself, in her disintegrating web of words. For although her webs disintegrate as quickly as she weaves them, Discordia is a weaver of sorts as well, as the language of the passage indicates. The repetition of *plex* in *simplex* and *duplex* recalls the *multiplici . . . strage* (line 686), "manifold slaughter," of the battlefield, where she hid her torn robe and whip before assuming her deceptive disguise. The repetition of the *plic* root hints at her connection with the dangerous side of weaving imagery, the cunning snare and the net, instruments of complicated deceit.

Discordia's speech reveals an underlying dynamic of the *Psychomachia*. From one point of view, the speech violates the sense of the narrative—it is difficult to accept that Discordia, whose very nature is to be ambiguous and deceptive, would deliver such a straightforward and honest description of her-

[13]*Aen.* 6.201–204: "inde ubi venere ad fauces grave olentis Averni, / tollunt se celeres liquidumque per aera lapsae / sedibus optatis gemina super arbore sidunt, / discolor unde auri per ramos aura refulsit" (Then, when they had come to the jaws of Avernus with its heavy vapors, they swiftly rise and, gliding through the clear air, they rest in their chosen perches above the double-natured tree, from which a strange-colored aura of gold shone through the branches). Vergil's choice of adjective for the golden bough is, as so often, motivated by wordplay. Pluto, lord of the underworld, gets his name (wealth) from the gold and other precious stones and metals that lie beneath the earth. One of Pluto's other names is *Dis;* the bough, which is made of gold, is thus Dis's color.

self, and yet she does. Her speech is not deceptive, but it is nevertheless characteristic of her nature. Instead of trying to maintain her disguise, Discordia chooses an even more radical and unsettling move: she tries to undermine language by revealing its arbitrary nature. It is no wonder that Fides, the leader of the Virtues and the one most concerned with the language of truth, is unable to endure Discordia's speech and tries to stop her appropriation of language by transfixing her tongue, the instrument of ambiguity, with her spear:

> non tulit ulterius capti blasphemia monstri
> Virtutum regina Fides, sed verba loquentis
> impedit et vocis claudit spiramina pilo,
> pollutam rigida transfigens cuspide linguam. |
> <div align="right">(<i>Ps.</i> 715–718)</div>

Unable to endure the captive monster's blasphemies any longer, Faith, queen of the Virtues, cut off Discordia's words as she spoke, closing off her vocal chords with a javelin and then transfixing her polluted tongue with a rigid spear.

By stopping Discordia's tongue, Fides attempts to prevent her polysemous punning and her dissemination of ambiguity.[14] The verse echoes this effort to achieve clarity in another golden line (718), this one with the pattern adjective, adjective, verb, noun, noun, but the effort is in vain. The Virtues kill Discordia, to be sure, but instead of enclosing her and containing her dangerous force, they, in their fury, rip her body to pieces and disseminate it through each of the three realms: earth, air, and sea. Discordia's death echoes Claudian's description of the death of Rufinus, and as in that passage, there is a reversal of roles at the moment of death. The Virtues,

[14]There is, perhaps—if we can agree with Frederick Ahl's contention that double letters, though separately pronounced, can be resolved into a single letter for the purpose of anagrammatic wordplays—another bilingual pun operating here. Discordia's tongue is *pollutam*, polluted, because she cannot stick to one meaning, as if *pollutam* were derived from Greek *polu*, "many." See Ahl, *Metaformations: Soundplay and Wordplay in Ovid and Other Classical Poets* (Ithaca, N.Y., 1985), pp. 56–57.

imbued with their opponent's divisive nature, become agents of dismemberment and dissolution.

This is not a random echo on Prudentius' part. Discordia's death is the climax of the *Psychomachia* and thus carries great thematic significance. Furthermore, it is unlikely that any of Prudentius' contemporaries would have missed an allusion to a recent event as important and as well publicized as Rufinus' spectacular assassination. There is at the very least a heavy irony in Prudentius' decision to use Rufinus' death as the model for the death of Discordia *cognomento Heresis,* and it is an irony that saps the foundations of any "straight" interpretation of the *Psychomachia.* For Rufinus, whatever his other character defects may have been, was, as we have noted, a pious orthodox Christian well known for his persecution of heretics. To find him the model for the personification of Heresy, and at the very climax of Prudentius' poem, calls for some explanation.

But indeed the unexpected allusion to Rufinus and the strange reversal of roles between Virtues and Vice at the moment of Discordia's death are part of a pattern that runs throughout the *Psychomachia.* The relationship between the Virtues and the Vices is consistently problematic. As Georgia Nugent remarks, "Just as on the narrative level the poem unmasks from time to time the myth that *virtus* and *vitium* are neat polarities, so linguistically *virtus* is not irrevocably fixed as one stable term in a polar opposition but can mediate between virtue and vice, expressing the powers of either."[15] Throughout the poem Prudentius makes it clear that the Virtues and the Vices have at least one thing in common: *vis,* or "force." *Virtus,* in one of its more general meanings (strength or force) is used to describe both the Virtues and the Vices, and this common name shows their fundamental similarity. They are not so much opposing moral categories as opposing *forces.* Though the battles maintain the fiction of ending consistently in decisive victory for the Virtues, one finds on closer inspection that Vice and Virtue exchange roles. To conquer a given

[15]Nugent, "Vice and Virtue in Allegory," p. 71.

Vice, the opposing Virtue must adopt some of her characteristics. One example serves particularly well. When Superbia (Pride) has fallen into a trap, her opponent, Mens Humilis (Humility), stands by the pit, smiling modestly and assuming a friendly expression hardly (as has been pointed out) appropriate to the occasion: *os quoque parce erigit et comi moderatur gaudia vultu.* She appears content to watch her enemy writhing at the bottom of the pit with a broken leg until Spes (Hope) comes forward to urge her on to the kill. Spes brings with her a sword—and something else:

> cunctanti Spes fida comes succurrit et offert
> ultorem gladium laudisque inspirat amorem.
> *(Ps. 278–279)*

> As she hesitates, her faithful companion Hope runs up to help, and offers her a sword of vengeance, breathing into her the love of glory.

Laudis amor, the fatal desire for glory that brings so many Vergilian heroes to their deaths, is an attribute that surely belongs by rights to Superbia, not her humble opponent. It is not until she has absorbed this dangerous desire that Mens Humilis can bring herself to cut off her opponent's head.

Thus, though the two armies oppose each other, they are not polar opposites. There is a middle ground of ambiguity where Vices and Virtues meet and are difficult to distinguish, expressed in the text by such puzzling events as the Vices claiming to possess *virtus,* and Mens Humilis propelled into violent action by the lust for fame. The same sort of opposition, in which the identities of the opponents are partially merged even though one is annihilated, is operating in the battle between Concordia and Discordia. This final battle is fought out on a topological middle ground. It takes place on the threshold of the camp, somewhere between the inside, the realm of Concordia, and the unlimited outside, the realm of Discordia, who knows no limits. That the enemies have something in common is emphasized by a point embedded in the most literal level of the text. If we strip both Concordia and Discordia of their prefixes and suffixes, we find the same root at the center of their names: COR, "heart." Concordia and Discordia, in their ambivalent relationship to one another, epitomize the battle in the heart that is the *Psychomachia*'s subject. In the tradition of Latin epic, which finds all civil wars ultimately self-destructive, we find in the desperate struggle of the Virtues to overcome the Vices a peculiar exchange of attributes between victor and vanquished. Just as Rufinus' attackers descended to the level of animals as a result of their vicious hatred of him, so the Virtues assimilate the disintegrating force of Discordia which they have been fighting against. Thus the stage is set for yet another cycle of this brutal war.

The poem ends in apparent harmony, with the establishment of a temple to Christ. Yet the possibility for further conflict is there. Discordia's disguise, so much like the disguises of Allecto and Laius, points to that possibility. Allecto and Laius are catalysts of wars that spin out of control, ominous precedents for this battle. Furthermore, the allusion to Rufinus removes the battle between orthodoxy and heresy from the realm of the purely abstract to the issues of Prudentius' own day, anchoring the poem for the first time in contemporary history. To find Rufinus the model for political discord is not surprising, but to find him the model for heresy is paradoxical, and it is this paradox that points to one of the deeper issues of the poem.

Prudentius and Claudian seem to interpret the death of Rufinus in similar ways. Claudian appreciates the irony of the persecutor persecuted, as we see from his beast-in-the-arena simile, and condemns Rufinus even in death for spreading violence throughout society. Prudentius uses Rufinus as his model for Heresy to point to the same issues. We must remember that persecution of heretic Christians was a new development in the late fourth century, and one that was not greeted with enthusiasm by all Christians, orthodox or otherwise. Many saw it as a policy that was tearing the church apart— Martin of Tours, a man of impeccable orthodoxy, tried to

intervene on behalf of Priscillian and his followers in one of
the earliest cases of government suppression of heresy. It is at
least conceivable that Prudentius, by modeling Discordia on
Rufinus and recalling his physical dismemberment at the
hands of a mob of angry soldiers, was implicitly criticizing not
only Rufinus, but also the government policy of religious intol-
erance Rufinus worked so hard to implement for Theodosius.
For Prudentius, though a Christian, was not an intolerant one:
he even made a plea to Honorius to allow pagan statues and
temples to stand unharmed and used the dead Theodosius as
his mouthpiece.

Thus the final battle of the *Psychomachia* ends in a Pyrrhic
victory for the Virtues. Discordia, though she appears to end
the conflict by her defeat in the seventh and apparently conclusive battle of the poem, nevertheless takes her place beside
Allecto and the ghost of Laius as a catalyst, spreading violence
and disruption into the army of the Virtues. The stage is set
for the battle in the soul to continue at a new level of intensity—and as we shall see in the next section, the battle in the
soul is only a small-scale model of chaos and confusion on the
larger levels of the state and the cosmos.

Civil Discord

Prudentius' Discordia is not entirely his own invention. The
personification of Discordia is something of a topos in Latin
epic poetry, and the imagery of binding and weaving which
Prudentius associates so strongly with both Concordia and
Discordia has a clearly traceable origin in Stoic philosophy and
poetry. We will look first at Discordia as she appears in the
Aeneid and in Petronius' *Bellum civile,* where she is an emblem
of civil strife, and then we will consider the Stoic image of the
binding of the cosmos, which was adopted and reversed by
Lucan, Manilius, and Prudentius himself.

Despite Prudentius' decision to locate the *Psychomachia* in a
world outside of history, his poem is not without political

overtones, as we have seen. The allusion to Rufinus' death, which must have been an extremely dramatic political event, anchors the poem in time and suggests that Prudentius' model of civil war in the soul reflected the civil and religious strife that was straining the resources of the empire to the breaking point in Prudentius' day. Discordia, though certainly associated with Heresy in the *Psychomachia,* is above all else a *political* figure in earlier epics. In the *Aeneid* she appears as one of the figures from Roman history which adorn Aeneas' shield:

> . . . saevit medio in certamine Mavors
> caelatus ferro, tristesque ex aethere Dirae,
> et scissa gaudens vadit Discordia palla,
> quam cum sanguineo sequitur Bellona flagello.
>
> > (*Aen.* 8.700–703)

> In the middle of the battle rages the war god Mars, carved in steel, and sorrow-making Dirae from heaven, and Discord in her torn robes strides along rejoicing, while Bellona follows with her bloody whip.

Discordia and her companions—the Dirae, Mars, and Bellona—are at the center of Vulcan's depiction of Actium, the final battle of Rome's bloody civil war. She has the torn cloak, which she discards in favor of a disguise in Prudentius' poem, but the whip she carries belongs here to Bellona, who follows her into battle.

Discordia is given a larger role, with a speaking part, in Petronius' *Bellum civile,* which appears to be a parody of Lucan's *Pharsalia.*[16] The poem, which describes the Roman civil war, is going to be a *proper* epic, as its narrator carefully explains beforehand, with *ambages* (digressions) and plenty of divine machinery (unlike Lucan's poem, which does have digressions, but which lacks gods). Discordia is only one of a number of personified figures and interfering deities in the

---

[16]See F. Baldwin's edition of the *Bellum civile* (New York, 1911); P. Grimal, *La guerre civile de Petrone dans ses rapports avec la pharsale* (Paris, 1977).

poem, which features appearances by Dis, Mars, Fors, and Fama, among others. Petronius gives a far more elaborate description of the goddess' appearance than Vergil does:

> Intremuere tubae ac scissa Discordia crine
> extulit ad superos Stygium caput. Huius in ore
> concretus sanguis, contusaque lumina flebant,
> stabant aerati scabra rubigine dentes,
> tabo lingua fluens, obsessa draconibus ora,
> atque inter torto laceratam pectore vestem
> sanguineam tremula quatiebat lampada dextra.
>
> (*B.C.* 271–277)

The trumpets wavered. Discord, her hair all torn, raised her hellish head to the heavens. Blood was scabbed on her face; her bruised eyes oozed with tears; her brassy teeth stood covered in scaly rust. Her tongue drooled rot; her face was besieged by snakes. A torn and bloody garment covered her twisted breast, and her trembling hand brandished a torch.

Her mission, like that of Allecto in *Aeneid* 7, is to stir Italy into civil war, and she barks out orders to the chief political figures of the day, including Caesar, Curio, and Pompey:

> "Tu legem, Marcelle, tene. Tu concute plebem,
> Curio. Tu fortem, ne supprime, Lentule, Martem.
> Quid porro tu, dive, tuis cunctaris in armis,
> non frangis portas, non muris oppida solvis
> thesaurosque rapis? Nescis tu, Magne, tueri
> Romanos arces? Epidamnia moenia quaere
> Thessalicosque sinus humano sanguine tingue."
> Factum est in terris quicquid Discordia iussit.
>
> (*B.C.* 288–295)

"Cling to your legalities, Marcellus; Curio, strike at the common people. Lentulus, don't try to suppress the war god's force. And you, divine one, why are you holding back your weapons? Why don't you break down the gates, shatter the town walls, and carry away the spoils? And you, great Pompey, have you forgotten how to defend the Roman citadel? Then go to the walls of Epidamnus and dye Thessalian harbors red with human blood." And all that Discord ordered was done on earth.

This Discordia is a ludicrously overdrawn figure, with her bruised and weeping eyes, blood-smeared face, and rusty teeth, but her role in the parody as the instigator of civil strife shows that her image as an icon of civil war was so common as to be a cliché. Prudentius has borrowed this highly politicized figure from the earlier poets and used her to represent strife on the microcosmic level of the soul. But by her very appearance, and by the similarity of her death to that of the once powerful politician Rufinus, he reminds us that Rome could not, in his day, shed the divisive legacy of civil war. The strife between brothers which marked Rome's birth still plagued the empire more than a thousand years later.

Cosmic Discord

The final battle of the *Psychomachia* is connected, through poetic allusions and elaborate imagery, not only to the political theme of civil war, but also to philosophic speculations about the destruction of the cosmos. Concordia's armor and Discordia's dress form an iconographic representation of a metaphor that pervades Prudentius' poetry and was widespread in later Latin literature. This is the metaphor of cosmic binding, which Michael Lapidge has traced from the Stoic philosopher Chrysippus through Cicero, Manilius, and Lucan, to the church fathers and the poets of Late Antiquity.[17]

According to Chrysippus, the matter that makes up the cosmos is permeated by a fiery substance (*pneuma*, breath), which, by its movement in the mass of matter, creates a "pneumatic tension" (*pneumatikos tonos*) that holds the universe to-

[17]Michael Lapidge, "A Stoic Metaphor in Late Latin Poetry: The Binding of the Cosmos," *Latomus* 39 (1980):817–837. Much of what follows is a summary of Lapidge's article.

gether and keeps the elements from disintegrating. He called
this tension a bond (*desmos*). Cicero, recapitulating his theory
in *De natura deorum,* translates *desmos* as *vinculum* (chain).[18]
The Latin poets adopted the metaphor of the bond or chain as
an image of cosmic harmony. Lucan shifts his emphasis from
the bonds that maintain the universe to the universal destruction that arises when the bonds are broken. In this evocative
passage from *Pharsalia* 1, he imagines the catastrophic Roman
civil war as an event that loosens the bonds of the cosmos and
plunges the entire physical universe into chaos:

> invida fatorum series summisque negatum
> stare diu nimioque graves sub pondere lapsus
> nec se Roma ferens. sic, cum compage soluta
> saecula tot mundi suprema coegerit hora,
> antiquum repetens iterum chaos, omnia mixtis
> sidera sideribus concurrent ignea pontum
> astra petent, tellus extendere littora nolet
> excutietque fretum, fratri contraria Phoebe
> ibit et obliquum bigas agitare per orbem
> indignata diem poscet sibi, totaque discors
> machina divolsi turbabit foedera mundi.
> in se magna ruunt: laetis hunc nomina rebus
> crescendi posuere modum.
>
> (*Phars.* 1.70–82)

It was a thread spun by the jealous fates; a fall from the heights
where no one stands for long; a terrible collapse under an impossible weight: it was Rome, unable to bear the burden of
herself. So, when the fabric of the universe is dissolved and the
world's last hour puts an end to the ages, the constellations will
collide, star upon star, seeking to drown their fires in the sea.
The earth will roll up her flat shores and shake off the waters of
the sea; the moon, shamed by her chariot's oblique path, will
defy her brother and demand the day for herself; and the whole
disheartened, disjointed machine of the shattered universe will

---

[18]Cicero *De natura deorum* 2.115: *quasi quodam vinculo circumdato colligantur*
(they are bound together as if surrounded by a kind of chain).

turn upon its own laws and break them. Great things are ruined
from within—the gods have put a limit on success.

For Lucan, the dissolution of the microcosmic bond of human
society is the first break in the chain, the beginning of an
unstoppable plunge into universal chaos and confusion.[19]

The idea of the bond that maintains universal harmony was
congenial to Christian writers as well as to Stoics. The Christians adopt the notion that God maintains order through the
bond of *philia*, love, and they accept Philo's notion that the
name of the Lord (*despotes*) is derived from *desmos*, bond, because it is God who binds the universe together and keeps it in
harmony. Prudentius, in another of his poems, the *Hamartigenia*, or "Origin of Sin," takes up the motif of cosmic bond-
ing at length in a passage that strongly recalls Lucan's picture
of universal dissolution:

> ipsa quoque oppositum destructo foedere certo
> transcendunt elementa modum rapiuntque ruuntque
> omnia legirupis quassantia viribus orbem.
> frangunt umbriferos aquilonum proelia lucos,
> et cadit immodicis silva exstirpata procellis. . . .
> nec tamen his tantam rabiem nascentibus ipse
> conditor instituit, sed laxa licentia rerum
> turbavit placidas rupto moderamine leges.
> nec mirum si membra orbis concussa rotantur,
> si vitiis agitata suis mundana laborat
> machina, si terras luis incentiva fatigat.
> exemplum dat vita hominum, quo cetera peccent.
>   (*Ham.* 236–240, 244–250)

Once the alliance is shattered, the elements themselves exceed
their limits. All things hurtle into ruin; the energy released from
the broken laws shakes the universe. The battling winds snap the
shady trees of the forest, and the whole wood comes crashing
down, uprooted by the limitless power of the storm. . . . But the

[19]Frederick M. Ahl, *Lucan: An Introduction* (Ithaca, N.Y., 1976), p. 242,
discusses this passage briefly.

Creator himself planted no such wrath in the world at its birth. Freedom, too much freedom threw the peaceful laws into turmoil and shattered all restraint. No wonder the stunned planet is sent spinning; no wonder the great machine of the universe, driven from within by its own flaws, staggers and strains, and a burning wave of corruption beats upon the lands! It is man who sets the pattern for the world's sins.

Here the elements break their bonds and shake the universe, causing a universal tempest. Prudentius' description of the forest uprooted by the blasts of storm winds is a metaphor for the destruction of the universe, a metaphor based on etymology, for *silva,* the word for forest, is a translation of the Greek *hule,* which means both "wood" (or "forest") and "matter." Servius, commenting on *Aeneid* 1.314, says:

> quam Graeci hulen vocant, poetae nominant silvam, id
> est elementorum congeriem unde cuncta procreantur.

What the Greeks call *hule,* the poets call *silva* (wood), that is, the gathering of elements from which all things are created.

Master Binders: God and the Poet

The collapsing bonds of the universe are mirrored in the apparent disintegration of Prudentius' own verse in the passage just quoted from the *Hamartigenia.* Immediately before the passage, Prudentius placed the line *pabula lascivis dederit sincera capellis.* This is a perfect golden line, with the symmetrical arrangement noun, adjective, verb, adjective, noun. In the verses that follow, describing the chaos of the universe, he repeatedly uses five-word lines, but he never quite manages to come up with another that has a verb in the middle balancing a pair of words on either side in symmetrical arrangement. For example, in line 246, *turbavit placidas rupto moderamine leges,* the verb *turbavit* is at the beginning of the line instead of the middle and thus disturbs the orderly progress of the verse as

75

much as its subject, *laxa licentia rerum,* disturbs the peaceful laws of the universe. The obvious parallel between the collapse of the universe and the collapse of the poet's verse suggests a parallel between the two creators, God and poet. The metaphor of binding which Prudentius applies to God is also his metaphor for poetic creation. In *Cathemerinon* 3, for example, he speaks of his poems as a wreath or crown:

> sperne, Camena, leves hederas,
> cingere tempora quis solita es,
> sertaque mystica dactylico
> texere docta liga strophio,
> laude Dei redimita comas.
>
> *(Cath.* 3.26–30)

Muse, put away the light ivy you use to crown your brow. Learn to weave mystic garlands and bind them with a ribbon of dactyls; decorate your hair with praise of God.

Here Prudentius picks up an ancient topos, one that goes back at least as far as Pindar's *Odes.* The poet wins a double crown: the first is in token of his mastery of the art of weaving verses, and the second is the verse itself, thought of as a woven crown of flowers that will never fade. The notion of the poet as master of the power of binding and weaving was an essential part of Prudentius' poetic persona and is a dominant motif in his *Peristephanon* ("On the Crowns").

Yet despite its associations with divine creation and the production of poetry, weaving and binding imagery is not uniformly benign in Prudentius' poetry. In his *Preface,* for example, Prudentius uses the metaphor of cosmic binding to describe God's creative powers, but the harmony of the universe does not necessarily bode well for the poet:

> per quinquennia iam decem
> ni fallor, fuimus; septimus insuper
> annum cardo rotat, dum fruimur sole volubili.

instat terminus, et diem
    vicinum senio iam Deus adplicat.

                      (*Praef.* 1–5)

I have lived, if I'm not deceived, for five decades now. On top of that, the turning world spins a seventh year, while I enjoy the swift sun. The end presses upon me, and the day God weaves now is close to old age.

The beginning of the poem is about time. Prudentius describes the spinning of the sun and the turning of the vault of the sky in words that suggest the inevitable turning of the Fates' spindle. After the turning and spinning imagery, we find God at work weaving the fabric of space and time—but, significantly, what he weaves for the poet is old age and death. Spinning and weaving, though creative, are at the same time binding forces, and Prudentius longs for release and freedom. He closes the poem with this wish:

haec dum scribo vel eloquor
    vinclis o utinam corporis emicem
    liber, quo tulerit lingua sono mobilis ultimo.
                  (*Praef.* 43–45)

As I write and speak these things, I wish I could flash forth, free of the chains of the flesh, to where my mobile tongue would guide me with its final note.

In this final verse, Prudentius' poetry becomes the potential instrument of his liberation. He would follow his tongue and transcend the bonds that restrain him: the poetic book, *liber,* which this preface introduces, will make him *liber,* free.[20]

Returning now to the *Psychomachia,* we can better understand the paradoxical force of the binding and weaving imagery in the poem's final battle. Concordia's armor, as closely woven as a garment can be, marks her as a representative of

[20]For a similar play on *līber* and *lĭber,* see Ovid *Tristia* 1.1.

the powerful force shared by God and the poet himself, who hopes to use the power of binding as an instrument of release. Concordia's strangely martial appearance (one would expect her to be the most peaceful of the Virtues) and the bristling, unpleasant sound of the verses that describe her armor, alert us to the ambiguity of this force, which can be either harmonious and creative or violent and repressive. Discordia represents the equally powerful force of dissolution and disintegration, a negative force in the context of the *Psychomachia,* but with its positive side as well, for it can be a means of liberation and release from bondage. The tension between the two forces, and between the conflicting values that can be ascribed to each, is dramatically played out in the final battle of the *Psychomachia.* But the reversal of roles between Virtues and Vices, the association of Discordia with figures who begin rather than end epic cycles of violence, and the disintegration of language we witness in the final battle lead us to question the apparently peaceful resolution of conflict at the end of the poem. In the chapters that follow, we shall see how Prudentius develops some of the themes suggested in this discussion. Binding and dismemberment are important images in his portrayal of the Christian Saint Hippolytus, whose death by dismemberment is based in part on the death of Rufinus and on Prudentius' own description of the death of Discordia. Tracing this imagery through the poems about Hippolytus, Cyprian, and Agnes will enable us to learn much about Prudentius' poetic technique and will shed some light upon his manipulation of myth, history, and the poetic tradition.

4

A Mythical Martyr

The *Psychomachia* is a world deliberately removed from history, its characters abstract and its geography vague. Prudentius stripped away all but the most essential underpinnings from the poem, and as a result the *Psychomachia* is in some ways the most easily comprehensible of all his poems, for it is the one in which he is most explicit about his manipulation of language. The world of the *Peristephanon* is very different and far more complex. In it Prudentius makes an audacious attempt to demonstrate the interpenetration of pagan mythology and Christian cult. The more closely his martyrs are examined, the less Christian they seem. In fact, as I will demonstrate below, Prudentius' versions of their martyrdoms do not always correspond to the accepted hagiographic tradition. He exercises the poet's freedom to alter not only details, but also basic elements and even identities. He is particularly fond of conflating the legends of people who bear the same name, even when he is well aware that the two belong to entirely separate traditions and have nothing in common except their names. In fact, Prudentius treats his saints as Vergil and Ovid treated the gods and heroes of Roman myth and tradition, with the same willingness to alter, adapt, and invent to suit his own poetic purposes.

Peristephanon 11 describes the death of Saint Hippolytus, a schismatic priest who, in the version of the story Prudentius tells, returned to orthodoxy and died a martyr's death. The poem is set in Rome at the saint's shrine in the catacombs of the Via Tiburtina. Prudentius' treatment of his sources in this poem is one of the clearest examples of his combining different traditions into a single version. The traditions about Saint Hippolytus are confused and confusing, so that on the face of it, it is not surprising to find some confusion in Prudentius' poem.[1] It is impossible to state with any certainty who Saint Hippolytus was, where he was from, or whether he is one person or an amalgamation of two or more. Yet we can establish certain fixed points:

1. A Hippolytus, living in the early third century, wrote a number of still extant theological treatises.

2. A Hippolytus, said to be a priest, was exiled along with Pontianus, the bishop of Rome, to Sardinia in 235, and is believed to have died as a result of his exile.

3. A bishop Hippolytus is named as a martyr by Jerome, who, regrettably, specifies neither his see nor the manner of his death.

4. A martyrium to Hippolytus was excavated just outside Rome on the Via Tiburtina in Renaissance times, and a statue of a seated figure was found. On the seat are carved the titles of Hippolytus' treatises. The statue, however, has recently been shown to be a sculpture of a woman, probably of a female Epicurean philosopher: the male head was added in the Renaissance. The treatises are thought to have been carved onto the already existing statue in the third century by Christians who took the statue to be a generic representation of Wisdom.[2]

[1]See John Francis Petrucione, "Prudentius' Use of Martyrological Topoi in *Peristephanon*," diss., University of Michigan, 1985, pp. 71–99, for a good summary of the evidence about Saint Hippolytus; P. Tino Alberto Sabattini, "Storia e leggenda nei *Peristephanon* di Prudenzio," *Rivista di studi classici* 20 (1973):187–221; Vicenzo Loi, "La problematica storico-letteraria su Ippolito di Roma," pp. 9–16; Pasquali Testini, "Di alcune testimonianze relative a Ippolito," pp. 45–63, both in *Ricerche su Ippolito,* Studia Ephemeridis Augustinianum (Rome, 1977); Gabriel Bertonière, *The Cult Center of the Martyr Hippolytus on the Via Tiburtina* (Oxford, 1985).

[2]Margherita Guarducci, "La statua di 'Sant' Ippolito,'" in *Ricerche su Ippolito,* pp. 17–30.

5. The shrine contains an epigram by the fourth century Pope Damasus, which asserts that Hippolytus was a priest who followed the Novatian schism for a time but returned to the faith and died a martyr. He does not specify the manner of the saint's death.[3]

Recent excavations in Ostia have uncovered another shrine from the early fourth century, which is also a martyrium, dedicated by Heraclidas, bishop of Porto. There are, then, two shrines, both claiming to hold the remains of Hippolytus and both in the vicinity of Rome. A conference held at the Vatican to try to straighten out this profusion of evidence resulted in the publication of a series of papers whose authors hypothesize that there were actually two writers named Hippolytus in the early third century.[4] One was in Rome in the early part of the third century, was exiled in 235, and probably died as a result of his exile. The other was bishop of an Eastern see who was active from the end of the second to the beginning of the third century.

It is difficult to piece together a coherent story. Prudentius' poem is one of the most important early sources of information on Hippolytus, but the most striking feature of his description of the martyrdom remains unattested in earlier accounts—his assertion that the saint was martyred by being tied to a team of horses who were driven off in opposite directions. This death corresponds suspiciously well to the saint's name: the popular etymology for Hippolytus derives it from the Greek *hippos*, horse, and *luo*, to loosen. Vergil shows his awareness of this etymology when he describes the mythical Hippolytus with the phrase *distractus equis* (torn apart by horses) (*Aen.* 7.767). A later text, the anonymous *Passio Polychronii* (probably from the end of the fifth century), attributes this same gruesome form of death to yet another Hippolytus, this one a

---

[3] All scholars who have examined the historicity of Hippolytus have agreed on chronological grounds that Damasus must be wrong about Hippolytus' adherence to the Novatian schism. Testini, "S. Ippolito," p. 45, argues that Damasus may have invented the accusation for political reasons, wishing, in an era rife with heresy, to hold Hippolytus up as an example of a heretic who returned to orthodoxy and achieved martyrdom.

[4] The results are published in *Ricerche su Ippolito* (1977).

man assigned to guard the martyr Lawrence. Just before his own death, Lawrence converts Hippolytus to Christianity, and Hippolytus, together with his nurse and some companions, are martyred as well. It is possible that this text was influenced by Prudentius' poem, for reasons discussed later in this chapter.

Prudentius claims to have seen the death of his Hippolytus depicted on a fresco in the catacombs of the Via Tiburtina. He also makes it clear in the poem that he had read Damasus' epigram and borrowed from it the notion that Hippolytus had been a heretic who returned in the end to orthodoxy. His insistence on placing the site of Hippolytus' martyrdom in Ostia, while at the same time specifying that he was returned to Rome for burial (a detail that thoroughly confused editors of the poem until the shrine at Ostia was discovered), reveals that Prudentius knew of the two shrines' conflicting claims to hold the saint's body. Testini points out, I believe correctly, that Prudentius' account conflates not only these two seemingly contradictory cults, but also the story of the mythical Hippolytus, though we need not agree with his opinion that Prudentius felt obliged to retreat into the world of myth to resolve the contradictions in the evidence.[5]

We begin to see what might make Saint Hippolytus an appealing figure to Prudentius. The story of his heresy and the conflicting claims of the cults at Ostia and Rome make him an appropriate figure to represent the conflict between *concordia* and *discordia,* as we shall see below, but just as important is his name, which allows Prudentius to incorporate the mythical Hippolytus into his poem. This kind of wordplay on the etymological meaning of saints' names was popular in the Late Antique period. As Petrucione has shown, these etymological puns had a serious meaning—they were meant to demonstrate the importance of the identity conferred by baptism upon the convert, and became a fixed feature of martyrological encomiums. Thus we see Damasus punning on the name

[5]Pasquali Testini, "S. Ippolito all'isola sacra," *Rendiconti della Pontificia Accademia Romana d'Archeologia* 51 (1978), p. 45.

Felix, Augustine on the names Vincent and Agnes, and Prudentius himself on Stephen, Eulalia, Agnes, Hippolytus, Cyprian, and Peter.[6] The same sort of pun, but associating a
Christian with a figure from classical mythology because of a
similar name, occurs in the following epitaph, written by the
Christian Neoplatonist (and contemporary of Prudentius)
Manlius Theodorus for his sister, Manlia Daedalia, who before
her death dedicated herself to virginity:

> clara genus censu pollens et mater egentum,
>   virgo sacrata Deo Manlia Daedalia,
> quae mortale nihil mortali in pectore volvens,
>   quo peteret caelum semper amavit iter.
>
>   (*CIL* 5.6240)[7]

Famous because of her race, powerful because of her fortune,
and mother of the needy, Manlia Daedalia, a virgin consecrated
to God. Contemplating immortal thoughts in her mortal heart,
she always loved the path by which she sought heaven.

Daedalia's name inspires her brother to allude to the flight of
Daedalus as a symbol of the soul's flight to heaven.

Thus when Prudentius decides to take advantage of the
etymological pun in the name Hippolytus, he is able to exploit
the mythical resonance of the name as well; that he does so is
made clear by his description of the death of his martyred
saint, taken from various sources describing the death of the
mythical Hippolytus.[8] The mythical Hippolytus is the son of

[6]Petrucione, "Prudentius' Use of Martyrological Topoi," pp. 40ff and
p. 111, gives many examples of etymological wordplay in *encomia* to martyrs
and discusses Prudentius' puns on the Greek names Stephen, Agnes, Vincent, Eulalia, and Peter. For the latter, see also Paul Künzle, "Bemerkungen
zum Lob auf Sankt Peter und Sankt Paul von Prudentius (*Perist.* 12)," *Rivista
di Storia della Chiesa in Italia* 11 (1957):309–370.

[7]This passage is also discussed by John Matthews, *Western Aristocracies and
the Imperial Court: A.D. 364–425* (Oxford, 1975), pp. 218–219.

[8]For a discussion of classical sources on the death of Hippolytus, see
Charles Segal, "Senecan Baroque: The Death of Hippolytus in Seneca, Ovid,
and Euripides," *TAPhA* 114 (1984):311–326, and cf. Seneca's *Phaedra* 1069–
1070, 1082, 1089 for Prudentius' dependence on Seneca.

Theseus, the slayer of the Minotaur, and of the Amazon Hippolyte (or Antiope). He has the unusual distinction of being the only male in Greek and Roman myth who is celebrated for his chastity: he is a devoté of the virgin huntress Diana and rejects sex completely.

Unfortunately, his beauty makes him the object of his stepmother Phaedra's passion. While Theseus is away on a journey to the underworld, Phaedra declares her love for Hippolytus, but he violently rejects her. Theseus suddenly returns, and Phaedra tells him that Hippolytus has raped her. Theseus then curses his son. While Hippolytus is driving his chariot along the shore, a bull-like monster emerges from the sea and terrifies his horses. Hipplytus falls from the chariot, becomes tangled in the reins, and is torn apart by the horses. He is finally stopped by a tree trunk impaling his groin. The body is reassembled and then, as Ovid and Vergil tell the story, Diana and Aesclepius bring Hippolytus back to life. Diana changes his appearance and settles him in her groves in Italy, changing his name to Virbius, the "twice-born man."

Prudentius' description of the death of his saint Hippolytus resembles the myth in several respects, aside from the obvious similarity of their deaths. Saint Hippolytus is a priest; we can presume that, like his mythic counterpart, he is chaste. He is figuratively reborn when he turns from his heretical ways and takes up orthodoxy. Prudentius locates his saint's death by the seashore, where the mythical Hippolytus met his death. One of the striking elements of Seneca's *Phaedra,* the description of the retrieval and reassembling of Hippolytus' body, is repeated in Prudentius' poem: Saint Hippolytus' followers wander through the landscape retrieving bits of his body, even sponging up his spilled blood, and carefully put the limbs back together before removing the body to Rome for burial.

Prudentius claims his source for the martyrdom and reassembling of the body is a fresco on the wall of Hippolytus' tomb:

> exemplar sceleris paries habet inlitus, in quo
> multicolor fucus digerit omne nefas;

picta super tumulum species liquidis viget umbris
    effigians tracti membra cruenta viri.
rorantes saxorum apices vidi, optime papa,
    purpureasque notas vepribus impositas.
docta manus virides imitando effingere dumos
    luserat et minio russeolam saniem.
cernere erat ruptis conpagibus ordine nullo
    membra per incertos sparsa iacere situs.
addiderat caros gressu lacrimisque sequentes,
    devia quo fractum semita monstrat iter.
maerore attoniti atque oculis rimantibus ibant
    implebantque sinus visceribus laceris.
ille caput niveum complectitur ac reverendam
    canitiem molli confovet in gremio;
hic umeros truncasque manus et bracchia et ulnas
    et genua et crurum fragmina nuda legit.
palliolis etiam bibulae siccantur harenae,
    ne quis in infecto pulvere ros maneat.
si quis et in sudibus recalenti aspergine sanguis
    insidet, hunc omnem spongia pressa rapit.

(Perist. 11.123–144)

The wall holds a painted model of the crime; many-colored
paints lay bare the unspeakable. Drawn above the tomb in clear,
living color, the image traces the bloody limbs of a man dismembered. The jagged rock tips dripped blood, dear bishop. I saw
them, and read the crimson signs imprinted on the bushes. An
artist skilled in crafting imitation trees in bright emerald makes
mock blood from vermilion dye. You could see the limbs lying
scattered on the uncertain ground, joints broken, all the rules of
composition ignored. Later, the artist added the dear friends
who followed, weeping, along the twisted trail that marked Hippolytus' broken path. Stunned with sorrow, they went along with
searching eyes, filling the folds of their tunics with his ravaged
guts. One man embraces the snowy head and warms its reverend
whiteness in his soft breast. Another collects shoulders, severed
hands and arms, elbows, knees, and naked fragments of leg.
They even dry the sands with thirsty cloths, lest any bloody dew
remain in the stained dust. And if any blood from the hot shower
settles on the branches, they press a sponge to it and carry it all
away.

It is evident that the fresco Prudentius describes has as its subject the death of the mythical Hippolytus, as we shall see in a moment. Prudentius' description is an unusual example of ecphrasis, a poetic device extremely popular in antiquity. An ecphrasis is a digression that interrupts a narrative in order to describe an object or a work of art, and artists often used the device to comment in some way upon the framework of their own creations. Prudentius' ecphrasis is intriguing because it dissolves its own frame, erasing the distinction between the painting being described and the poem describing it. As Gabriel Bertonière, an archaeologist working on Hippolytus' tomb on the Via Tiburtina, has noticed, "the description of the painting is not only mentioned in the context of the narration, but serves as part of the narration itself, particularly in the part which describes the gathering of the martyr's members. In fact, one is not sure where the description of the painting ends and the thread of the story is taken up again."[9] By refusing to close the frame of the ecphrasis, Prudentius creates the impression that the painting contains everything in the rest of the poem, including the saint's tomb and even the poet himself, who later appears as a character contemplating the mirrored shrine in the center of the tomb. This lack of closure and suggestion of dissolving boundaries in a poem describing an ambivalent pagan-Christian figure is reminiscent of Ausonius' *Cupid Crucified,* in which Cupid assumes a Christ-like role. That poem is also elaborately framed, and as in *Peristephanon* 11, the description of the painting imperceptibly becomes the narrative of the poem.

The painting Prudentius describes is the medium that allows him to step from the world of Christian history to the world of classical myth, for the work of art forms a space where the two worlds meet. The painting is a standard and popular treatment of its classical subject: Philostratus the Elder describes an almost identical painting of the death of Hippolytus in his *Imagines:*

[9]Bertonière, *The Cult Center of the Martyr Hippolytus on the Via Tiburtina* (Oxford, 1985), p. 42.

The horses, as you see, scorning the yoke toss their manes unchecked, not stamping their feet like well-bred and intelligent creatures, but overcome with panic and terror, and spattering the plain with foam, one while fleeing has turned its head toward the beast, another has leaped up at it, another looks at it askance, while the onrush of the fourth carries him into the sea as though he had forgotten both himself and the dry land; and with erect nostrils they neigh shrilly, unless you fail to hear the painting. . . . And thou, O youth that lovest chastity, thou hast suffered injustice at the hands of thy stepmother, and worse injustice at the hands of thy father, so that the painting itself mourns thee. . . . Neither did thy courage protect thee nor yet thy strong arm, but of thy members some have been torn off and others crushed, and thy hair has been defiled with dirt; thy breast is still breathing as though it would not let go of the soul, and thine eye gazes at all thy wounds.[10]

Prudentius himself describes a similar painting of Hippolytus from the temple of Diana Trivia in the *Contra Symmachum,* his reply to Symmachus' famous speech requesting the restoration of the altar of Victory to the Senate.[11] The *Contra Symmachum* is, in addition to a condemnation of pagan theology, a lengthy discussion of the relationships between religion, politics, and art. In the passage below, which refers to the other Hippolytus fresco, Prudentius shows both an awareness of the problem of censorship and subtlety in dealing with it.[12] His approach is well illustrated by the long speech he

[10]From *Philostratus, Imagines; Callistratus Descriptions,* Eng. trans. by Arthur Fairbanks (Cambridge: Harvard University Press, Loeb Classical Library, 1960), 2.4.2–4.

[11]Because Symmachus proposed the restoration of the statue in 384 and Prudentius did not compose his poem until 402–403, it is clear that something other than Symmachus' speech inspired Prudentius to write the poem.

[12]Tony Honoré, *"Scriptor Historiae Augustae," JRS* 77 (1987):156–176, offers an analysis of the textual strategies employed by the unknown author of the *Historia Augusta* to criticize the emperor Theodosius' decision to make the young Honorius heir to the throne. This author's cryptic style and oblique approach are very similar to Prudentius'. Honoré argues convincingly that the author was a contemporary of Prudentius, dating the work to ca. 395; he also discusses the author's use of significant puns and etymological wordplays

attributes to the emperors Honorius and Arcadius, who ridicule the worship of the statue of Victory in the Senate and condemn art of all sorts. They are particularly opposed to the unholy alliance they see between religion, painting, and poetry, and it is in this context that they describe the Hippolytus painting:

> sic unum sectantur iter, sic inania rerum
> somnia concipiunt et Homerus et acer Apelles
> et Numa, cognatumque malum pigmenta, Camenae,
> idola, convaluit fallendi trina potestas.
> haec si non ita sunt, edatur, cur sacra vobis
> ex tabulis cerisque poetica fabula praestat?
> cur Berecyntiacus perdit truncata sacerdos
> inguina, cum pulchrum poesis castraverit Attin?
> cur etiam templo Triviae lucisque sacratis
> cornipedes arcentur equi, cum Musa pudicum
> raptarit iuvenem volucri per litora curru,
> idque etiam paries tibi versicolorus adumbret?
>
> (*CS* 2.45–56)

So Homer, fierce Apelles, and Numa all follow one path, so they beget empty dream worlds. Paints, Muses, and idols are related evils: together they create a strong triple power of deceit. If this isn't true then tell us why paintings and wax sketches of poet's tales are the things you hold sacred. Why does the priest of Cybele cut off his genitals, when poetry has castrated lovely Attis? And why are horn-footed horses barred from the temple and sacred groves of the goddess of the crossroads, when the Muse has captured the chaste youth in his chariot as it flies along the shore, and there is even a color painting on the wall to show it to you?

The speech is delivered by the young emperors, who somehow manage to speak simultaneously from *placidissima ora* (very peaceful lips) (*CS* 2.17–18), although one is in Rome and

---

as well as his habit of leaving "signposts" to draw attention to the parts of his narrative which he did not intend to be believed.

the other in Constantinople. Their argument is not subtle. The gods are dismissed as artistic creations foolishly worshipped by the people. Homer, Apelles, and, remarkably, Numa, are grouped together as dangerous men who created *inania rerum somnia,* "empty dream worlds."[13] Their insistence on placing Numa, one of the most respected figures of early Rome, in this group is curious. As Dumézil points out, Numa represents a type absolutely necessary for the city's survival:

> The reigns of Romulus and Numa were conceived as the two wings of a diptych, each of them demonstrating one of two types, one of the two equally necessary but antithetical provinces of sovereignty. Romulus is a young demigod, impetuous, creative, violent, unhampered by scruples, exposed to the temptations of tyranny; Numa is a completely human old man, moderate, an organizer, peaceful, mindful of order and legality.[14]

Numa is also, as Ovid shows in his *Fasti,* a man who knows how to manipulate words—which, as we shall see, is not a characteristic of Prudentius' emperors. With his cunning wordplay, Numa outwits Jupiter and finds an acceptable substitute for human sacrifice. In Ovid's interpretation of the Numa story, the replacement of human sacrifice with ritual substitutes is an essential step in the civilizing of human society.

Thus it is strange to find the emperors rejecting Numa, the archetype of the civilized and just ruler in Roman mythology. It is also strange to find them accusing Numa, Homer, and Apelles of following the same path (*sic unum sectantur iter*), when error and confusion are more usually represented in Prudentius' poetry as straying *away* from the one path along labyrinthine sideroads. The imperial criticism is at odds with Prudentius' own imagery elsewhere in his poems.

The emperor's arguments do not seem to reflect Pruden-

---

[13]This reading may be incorrect. See note 17 below.
[14]Dumézil, *Archaic Roman Religion,* trans. Philip Krapp (Chicago, 1970), p. 180.

tius' own views about art and society; indeed, in some respects, they are antithetical. The emperors call for the wholesale destruction of pagan artworks in their joint communiqué, suggesting that Rome should replace its art and literature with the trophies of conquest:

> Vis decorare tuum, ditissima Roma, senatum?
> Suspende exuvias armis et sanguine captas,
> congere caesorum victrix diademata regum,
> frange repulsorum foeda ornamenta deorum.
>
> (*CS* 2.61–64)

Rome, wealthiest of all cities, do you wish to decorate your senate? Conqueror, hang up spoils won by arms and blood; heap the diadems of slaughtered kings in piles, destroy the foul ornaments of the defeated gods.

Prudentius himself earlier in the poem makes a plea for the *preservation* of classical statues, which he places in the mouth of the previous emperor, Theodosius. The question of the destruction of pagan shrines and statues was a vexed one even during Theodosius' reign. The emperor's policy and the actions of his officials were sometimes at variance: Theodosius' supporters, especially Maternus Cynegius, were known for their attacks on pagan shrines.[15]

In *Contra Symmachum* 1.502–505 Prudentius seems at pains to stress Theodosius' tolerance of pagan art. Unlike his sons, Theodosius is generally a heroic character in Prudentius' poetry; there can be little doubt that in this case Prudentius is holding him up (perhaps ironically) as an exemplar of tolerance to be imitated by Honorius and Arcadius, who do not come off terribly well in this poem. As Prudentius portrays

[15]See Matthews, *Western Aristocracies*, pp. 132–145, for a longer discussion of the zealotry of Theodosius' Spanish and Gallic courtiers and their role in the destruction of temples at Apamea, Edessa, and Egypt. He cites the evidence of Libanius about the persecution of pagans and the destruction of pagan shrines near Antioch and quotes a law from the *Codex Theodosianus* (*CTh* 16.10.8) requesting the preservation of the temple at Edessa and confirming Prudentius' attribution of such a policy to Theodosius.

them, the young emperors are literalists. They wish to replace art with some form of trophy—the spoils of war or the crowns of slaughtered enemies. The selection of the diadems is telling: instead of the living garland of poetry, which is Prudentius' metaphor for his own verse, the emperors consider the metallic crowns of slaughtered kings to be the appropriate symbol of Rome. Their inability to interpret poetry and art correctly is betrayed by their unsophisticated use of language: they anticipate with confidence, for example, the death of kings, failing to notice that the words *caesorum . . . regum* (slaughtered kings) sound much like a description of their own position, *regum Caesarum*.[16] Their failure to understand the principles of artistic creation is suggested by another near pun: when they condemn Numa, Apelles, and Homer, they berate them for conceiving empty dreams of things, *inania rerum somnia*. It is hard to hear this phrase without thinking of Lucretius' *semina rerum,* the "seeds of things" that make up the universe. What are *somnia* to the emperors are *semina* to poets and artists, who use them to create their own kind of life in the living microcosm of literature.[17]

The emperors' criticism applies not only to pagan artists. The kind of art they condemn is Prudentius' own. The wall painting of Hippolytus being dragged behind his chariot which so offends the emperors reappears in *Peristephanon* 11, in which Hippolytus is strangely metamorphosed from pagan hero to Christian saint. In the Hippolytus poem, Prudentius

[16]See Frederick M. Ahl, *Metaformations: Soundplay and Wordplay in Ovid and Other Classical Poets* (Ithaca, N.Y., 1985), pp. 80–81, for more on the relationship between *Caesar* and *caedo.*

[17]This point must fall in the realm of the speculative. Not only is it impossible to *prove* a Lucretian allusion from the sound of a phrase, but the words in question are based on a contested reading. I prefer to go along with Lavarenne (Prudentius, *Oeuvres* [Paris, 1955]) in reading *sic inania rerum somnia,* despite the metrical difficulties, because there is strong manuscript evidence for it and because I find the Lucretian ring of the phrase appropriate to this passage. This is not a conclusive argument, however, and Maurice Cunningham (*Aurelii Prudentii Clementis Carmina,* Corpus Christianorum, Series Latinum, vol. 126 [Turnholt, 1966]), whose text is generally sound, rejects the reading in favor of *sic cassa figuris.*

has done exactly what the emperors condemn pagan artists for doing. He has drawn from mythology, from classical poetry, and from painting and has recombined the various elements into his own *poetica fabula,* describing a new hero worshipped by the people.[18]

Prudentius' Hippolytus, martyr though he is, is not an entirely positive figure in the poem. Prudentius exploits one element of the hagiographic tradition, which makes Hippolytus a reformed adherent of the Novatian schism, in order to associate him with the conflict between Heresy, Discordia's other name in the *Psychomachia,* and Concordia. Elsewhere in Prudentius' poetry, heresy (unpersonified) is described as a king of mental wandering from the right path, and is accompanied by the same sort of labyrinth imagery that plays a prominent part in *Peristephanon* 11.

Prudentius also uses the mythic Hippolytus' death by dismemberment to link his saint with Discordia's other aspect, violent dissolution. Hippolytus' death in this poem bears a striking resemblance to the death of Discordia in the *Psychomachia. Peristephanon* 11, the basic theme of which is discord, is in part a comment on the divisiveness that characterized the Christianity of Prudentius' day. By overtly syncretizing the Christian and pagan heroes, however, Prudentius points to another, even more dangerous example of discord—the attempt by the conservative and powerful Christian faction that dominated the imperial court from Theodosius' time to dis-

[18]As if to emphasize his use of classical sources in the Hippolytus passage, Prudentius describes the wall painting in *Contra Symmachum* 2 in lines that clearly echo Vergil's account of the death of Hippolytus in *Aeneid* 7: "unde etiam templo Triviae lucisque sacratis / cornipedes arcentur equi" (*Aen.* 7.778–779) (And so it is that horn-footed horses are still kept out of Trivia's temple and sacred groves); "cur etiam templo Triviae lucisque sacratis cornipedes arcentur equi" (*CS* 2.53–54) (Why are horn-footed horses still kept out of Trivia's temple and sacred groves?). Thus the Catholic emperors, who wish to eliminate all references to classical art and literature, are made to speak the language of the *Aeneid.* Prudentius ironically undercuts their message, as if to emphasize the impossibility of the sort of censorship they propose: if they conformed to their own standards of proper speech, they would effectively silence themselves.

sociate the church entirely from the pagan past. It seems
Prudentius found many aspects of Christianity fundamentally
similar to trends already well developed in the Roman religious and literary tradition.

It is, in a way, a tribute to the accuracy of his perception that
his basic point has gone unrecognized for so long. His adaptation of the Hippolytus myth was, indeed, so appropriate a
medium for expressing certain aspects of the Christian experience that his substantial borrowings from pagan myth have
attracted little attention. His poem demonstrates that myth,
that ancient and powerful medium of religious and philosophic experience, could not be simply abandoned and that
Christianity was not an alternative to it, but a part of the same
process. The Christian Hippolytus as Prudentius presents him
is thus not simply a reformed heretic martyr, but also the latest
incarnation of his durable pagan prototype. He embodies the
conflict between the force of dissolution and the force of binding so strikingly illustrated by his death.

In the next section we shall see how Prudentius uses a
sophisticated network of imagery and allusion to identify his
mythical martyr with the opposing forces of Discordia and
Concordia in the *Psychomachia* and how he uses two separate
but allied systems of imagery—violent dismemberment, and
deceitful snares and labyrinths—to evoke the bewildering
confusion exemplified by the wandering underground corridors of Hippolytus' tomb.

Hippolytus and Discordia

Prudentius' Hippolytus is not, as we have seen, a straightforward Christian saint. He is identified with the classical hero
Hippolytus by the painting Prudentius claims to have seen on
the wall of his tomb and by the striking similarity of their
deaths, which enact the meaning of their shared name. Imagery of binding and dissolution and careful allusions to other
poems associate Hippolytus with the figure of Discordia.

These, together with Prudentius' use of labyrinth imagery, which he uses to describe Hippolytus' heresy at the beginning of the poem and which he develops at length later in his description of the saint's tomb, form a constellation of thematic images that can help us interpret *Peristephanon* 11.

Hippolytus, as soon as he appears in the poem, is associated with heresy:

> haec dum lustro oculis et sicubi forte latentes
> rerum apices veterum per monumenta sequor,
> invenio Hippolytum, qui quondam scisma Novati
> presbyter attigerat, nostra sequenda negans.
>
> (*Perist.* 11.17–20)

As I tracked these with my eyes and hunted among the monuments for the traces of ancient letters which I thought might be lurking there, I discovered Hippolytus, a priest who once attached himself to the schism of Novatius and said that ours should not be followed.

Prudentius' information is not historically accurate; he has accepted the information contained in the epigram Pope Damasus had inscribed on the tomb. Accurate or not, however, the supposed heresy plays a determining role in Prudentius' portrayal of Hippolytus. Heresy, we may recall, was the other name of that most destructive of Vices in the *Psychomachia*, Discordia, who identifies herself to the Virtues who have taken her captive with this declaration:

> . . . illa,
> exsanguis turbante metu: "Discordia dicor,
> cognomento Heresis; Deus est mihi discolor," inquit,
> "nunc minor aut maior, modo duplex et modo simplex,
> cum placet, aerius et de phantasmate visus,
> aut innata anima est quotiens volo ludere numen;
> praeceptor Belia mihi, domus et plaga mundus."
>
> (*Ps.* 708–714)

White with whirling fear, she says: "I am called Discord. My other name is Heresy. My God is variable—sometimes small, sometimes huge; sometimes two, sometimes one. When I wish, he seems like an airy phantom; or when I want to play tricks with divine power, he is the inborn soul. Belial is my teacher, the world is my territory and my home."

Discordia, as I noted in the first chapter, is associated with ambiguity, disguise, and confusion, not simply with strife. She is characterized in the *Psychomachia* by the language and imagery of dissolution and disintegration, symbolized iconographically by her torn robe and whip, but she is also associated with the snares of deceit. In *Peristephanon* 11, we find a similar constellation of imagery clustered around the figure of Hippolytus, who dies in the same manner as Discordia, torn limb from limb, parts of his body scattered over the landscape. As in the final battle of the *Psychomachia*, *Peristephanon* 11 alternates between imagery of binding and imagery of disintegration, particularly in the description of the saint's punishment and death. It begins with a description of the torture and death of the group of Christians led by Hippolytus. They are torn apart with metal instruments; some of them are crucified and left to be devoured by birds, others decapitated, still others burned alive. But the most elaborate punishment is reserved for a group put out to sea on a leaky boat. Here the judge orders their punishment:

> En tibi quos properes rimosae imponere cumbae,
> pellere et in medii stagna profunda freti.
> quos ubi susceptos rabidum male suta per aequor
> vexerit et tumidis caesa labarit aquis.
> dissociata putrem laxent tabulata carinam,
> conceptumque bibant undique naufragium.
> squamea caenoso praestabit ventre sepulcrum
> belua consumptis cruda cadaveribus.
>
> (*Perist.* 11.69–76)

Look at these people! Hurry, put them on a leaky boat and drive it into the deep water where the waves are wild. The boat is held together by a thread; when it has carried them across the raging fields of the sea, the swollen waves will tear it apart and sink it.

The rotten hull's timbers will disintegrate, drunk with the ship's utter ruin. A scaly monster of the deep will appear and gorge on their corpses—his slimy belly will provide their grave.

Imagery of dissolution abounds: the Christians will be put on a leaky boat (*rimosae cumbae*, an allusion to Charon's leaky boat in *Aeneid* 6); the boat is badly fitted together (*male suta*); the waves will shatter it; the beams of the rotten hull will come apart; the Christians will be eaten by sea monsters.

Immediately following this barrage of imagery of dissolution, Hippolytus appears, and the language suggesting binding begins to predominate:

> haec persultanti celsum subito ante tribunal
> offertur senior *nexibus implicitus.*
> *stipati circum* iuvenes clamore ferebant
> ipsum christicolis esse caput populis.
>
> (*Perist.* 11.77–80)

The judge was giving his arrogant orders from the high tribunal, when suddenly an old man bound in chains was delivered to him. A crowd of youths surrounding him shouted that he was the head of the people who worshipped Christ.

The old man Hippolytus is tightly bound and, like Concordia just before she is attacked, he is surrounded by a crowd (*stipati circum iuvenes;* cf. *Concordia . . . stipata, Ps.* 670–671). The judge asks his name, and when told it is Hippolytus, decides to let his name decide his fate. Prudentius emphasizes that Hippolytus' name helps determine his fate, a principle found in other poems of the *Peristephanon.*[19] Before he is

[19]This is something of a topos for Hippolytus. Like Vergil, who translates Hippolytus into Latin as *distractus equis,* "torn apart by horses," Ausonius, in one of his epigrams, remarks that Hippolytus' name was an indication of his fate: "qui primus Meroe, nomen tibi condidit, ille / Thesidae nomen condidit Hippolyto. / nam divinare est, nomen componere, quod sit / fortunae et morum vel necis indicium" (*Epig.* 41.1–4) (The man who first named you, Meroe, also found the name for Theseus' son, Hippolytus. For it is prophecy, to find a name which indicates fate, or character, or death).

dismembered, however, the horses must be yoked, and Hippolytus must be bound to them. The ultimate dissolution is preceded by elaborate binding imagery:[20]

> iamque reluctantes sociarant vincula bigas,
> oraque discordi foedere nexuerant;
> temonis vice funis inest, qui terga duorum
> dividit, et medius tangit utrumque latus.
> deque iugo in longum se post vestigia retro
> protendens trahitur, transit et ima pedum.
> Huius ad extremum, sequitur qua pulvere summo
> cornipedum refugas orbita trita vias,
> crura viri innectit laqueus nodoque tenaci
> adstringit plantas cumque rudente ligat.
>
> (*Perist.* 11.95–104)

And now the struggling pair are tied together with chains and their bound heads make them reluctant allies. In place of the chariot pole is a rope, which separates their backs and touches both their flanks. From the yoke the rope extends a long way back, dragging along behind their footprints and reaching past their hooves. At the end of the rope, where the trail it marks in the deep dust follows the path left by the fleeing horses, a noose is woven around the old man's legs. A tenacious knot binds his feet and ties them to the rope.

This passage is as crowded with imagery of binding and weaving as the description of Concordia's armor in the *Psychomachia*, but there is a more obvious tension here between the binding imagery and the dissolution that threatens momentarily. The horses are struggling against their bonds (*reluctantes*); they are tied together in a discordant bond (*discordi foedere nexuerant*); the tight knots and ropes that bind the old man's legs will, we are about to discover, hold together better than his body.

The horses are finally driven apart, and the poem explodes into fragments:

[20]Cf. Sen. *Phaedra* 1086f.

prorumpunt alacres caecoque errore feruntur,
    qua sonus atque tremor, qua furor exagitant.
incendit feritas, rapit impetus et fragor urget,
    nec cursus volucer mobile sentit onus.
per silvas, per saxa ruunt, non ripa retardat
    fluminis, aut torrens oppositus cohibet;
prosternunt saepes et cuncta obstacula rumpunt,
    prona, fragosa petunt, ardua transiliunt.
scissa minutatim labefacto corpore frusta
    carpit spinigeris stirpibus hirtus ager.
pars summis pendet scopulis, pars sentibus haeret,
    parte rubent frondes, parte madescit humus.

(Perist. 11.111–122)

The keen horses burst out. Blind confusion carries them along
where noise, terror, and madness drive them. Wildness enflames
them; momentum siezes them; the din spurs them onwards.
They run so fast they cannot feel the burden that flies behind
them. Through woods, through fields they race. River banks
cannot slow them; torrents in their path cannot check them;
they flatten fences and break down any obstacles in their path.
They seek out steep and broken slopes and fly over hurdles. The
body is shattered and cut into tiny pieces which stick in the
thorny bushes of the bristling field. Part of it hangs from the
steep sharp rocks; part clings to brambles; part dyes leafy shoots
red; part soaks into the earth.

The body is completely dismembered, ripped into tiny
pieces (*scissa minutatim . . . frusta*) that cling to various features
of the landscape. In the *Psychomachia* we find the same emphasis on the scattering of the body:

frustatim sibi quisque rapit, quod spargat in auras,
quod canibus donet, corvis quod edacibus ultro
offerat, inmundis caeno exhalante cloacis
quod trudat, monstris quod mandet habere marinis.
discussum foedis animalibus omne cadaver
dividitur, ruptis Heresis perit horrida membris.

(Ps. 720–725)

Each siezes a piece for herself. They scatter the pieces in the air, give them to the dogs, and offer them to the hungry crows. They shove some pieces down into slime-breathing sewers of the underworld; they give some to the monsters of the sea. The whole dismembered corpse is divided among the carrion animals. So dies dreadful Heresy, her body completely torn asunder.

In the *Psychomachia,* as we saw in Chapter 3, death by dismemberment is an enactment of the divisive power of *discordia;* it is a punishment that exactly fits the crime. In the *Peristephanon,* Hippolytus is associated with the same divisive force, both overtly in the assertion of his heresy when he first appears in the poem, and more subtly, by the pervasive imagery of dissolution which permeates the poem. Discordia's end, however, is not the only model for Hippolytus' death. There is a scene on Aeneas' shield which resembles Prudentius' description of the painting of the dismemberment, and in this scene Vergil, too, uses dismemberment to symbolize divisiveness:

> haud procul inde citae Mettum in diversa quadrigae
> distulerant (at tu dictis, Albane, maneres!),
> raptabatque viri mendacis viscera Tullus
> per silvam, et sparsi *rorabant* sanguine *vepres.*
>
> > (*Aen.* 8.642–645)

Not far from here, chariots driven in different directions tore Mettus apart (but you, man of Alba, should have stayed true to your word!) and Tullus dragged the lying man's guts through the woods, and the bushes sparkled, sprinkled with the bloody dew.

Vergil is describing the death of Mettus (or Mettius) Fufetius, a king who broke his alliance with the Romans at a crucial moment in battle.[21] Livy describes Mettus' punishment and

---

[21]See Ahl's discussion (*Metaformations,* pp. 304–307) of Vergil's wordplays in this scene and his representation of Mettus as an exemplar of divided loyalties and ruptured *fides.*

says explicitly that his death was arranged to symbolize the crime he committed.[22] Both the Livy and the Vergil passages point out the congruity of the punishment and the crime. Mettus, because of his lack of *fides,* his deliberate shattering of the bond that should hold allies together, is punished by dismemberment, the physical destruction of the bonds holding the body together.

Hippolytus, then, is linked with a number of figures who represent the shattering of bonds in various ways: with Prudentius' own allegorical character, Discordia, and thus with Rufinus, and finally with the oath breaker Mettus, who, like Hippolytus, becomes the subject of a work of art. It remains to be seen, however, in what way the theme of *discordia* is relevant to the myth of Hippolytus, the son of Theseus. We now turn to the relationship between the imagery of dissolution, which symbolizes discord on so many levels in the poem, and the labyrinth imagery that shapes Prudentius' description of the saint's tomb and occurs elsewhere in his work as a symbol of the mind gone astray. But it is worth remarking at this point that the curious resemblance in imagery between the death of Saint Hippolytus in *Peristephanon* 11 and the battle between Concordia and Discordia in the *Psychomachia* may have left its mark on the shape of the Hippolytus legend in later years. The collection of martyrs' legends transmitted under the name *Passio Polychronii* includes the story of a Hippolytus (connected with Saint Lawrence, and not the schismatic cleric of *Peristephanon* 11), who, true to his name, was sentenced to be torn apart by horses.[23] In this tale, however, a gratuitous character

[22]"Metti Fufeti," inquit, "Si ipse discere posses fidem et foedera servare, vivo tibi ea disciplina a me adhibita esset; nunc, quoniam tuum insanabile ingenium est, at tuo dupplicio doce humanum genus ea sancta credere quae a te violata sunt. Ut igitur paulo ante animum inter Fidenatem Romanamque rem ancipitem gessisti, ita iam corpus passim distrahendum dabis" (Livy, 1.28.9–11) ("Mettius Fufetius," he said, "if you were able to learn loyalty and keep treaties, I would have taught you this lesson while you were alive, but now, since your nature is incurable, at least you will teach the human race, by the example of your punishment, to hold sacred the things which you violated. So, just as a little earlier your mind was divided between Fidenae and Rome, now you will give your body to be torn apart").

[23]See Hippolyte Delehaye, "Recherches sur le légendier romain," *Analecta*

turns up—an old and loyal nurse who follows Hippolytus to
martyrdom. It is hard to avoid thinking that the presence of
the nurse in this late fifth-century passion of Hippolytus is
attributable to the important role of the nurse in the drama of
Phaedra and Hippolytus. The appearance of the nurse suggests the lasting importance of the mythical paradigm in shap-
ing the various stories about martyrs named Hippolytus. But
even more relevant to this interpretation, which links Hippolytus to the figures of Concordia and Discordia, is that the
name of this other Hippolytus' nurse is *Concordia*. It is likely
that the author of the *Passio Polychronii* had read Prudentius; if
we can rule out sheer coincidence in the naming of the nurse,
perhaps we can conclude that he understood him as well.

Heresy and Error

Early in *Peristephanon* 11, Prudentius describes Hippolytus
just before his arrest and torture. He is an old man accompanied by a group of followers who ask him which of the
various and competing Christian sects ought to be followed.
Hippolytus firmly endorses orthodoxy, denouncing the Novatian schism, which he has now rejected, and thus saves his
followers from falling into error:

> his ubi detorsit laevo de tramite plebem
> monstravitque sequi, qua via dextra vocat,
> seque ducem recti spretis anfractibus idem
> praebuit, erroris qui prius auctor erat.
> *(Perist.* 11.35–38)

With these words he twisted his people from the left-hand path
and showed them how to follow where the right path called. He
offered to be their leader along the right way now that he had
rejected his turnings—he who had once been error's author.

Bollandiana 39 (1921):314–322, for the text of the *Passio Polychronii* and a
discussion of its probable date.

The saint's heretical actions are here described as a failure to follow the right path. Hippolytus is called the *auctor erroris,* as if he had invented the heresy he now rejects; the heresy itself is an *error,* both a mistake and a wandering. His old beliefs are called *spretis anfractibus,* "rejected turnings and twistings." Heresy and error (wandering) are one and the same thing; later in the poem, when Prudentius describes Hippolytus' dismemberment, the physical dissolution of the saint's body is linked with imagery of wandering (*error*) when Hippolytus' horses run wild:

> prorumpunt alacres caecoque errore feruntur,
> qua sonus atque tremor, qua furor exagitant.
> *(Perist.* 11.111–112)

The keen horses burst out. Blind confusion (or wandering, *error*) carries them along wherever noise, terror, and madness drive them.

The horses retrace Hippolytus' blind wanderings as they scatter his body about the countryside.

This association between imagery of dismemberment, wandering, and heresy is more fully developed in the preface to another of Prudentius' poems, the *Apotheosis:*

> Est vera secta? te, Magister, consulo.
> rectamne servamus fidem?
> an viperina non cavemus dogmata,
> et nescientes labimur?
> artam salutis vix viam discernere est
> inter reflexas semitas.
> tam multa surgunt perfidorum conpita
> tortis polita erroribus.
> obliqua sese conserunt divortia
> hinc inde textis orbitis.
> quas si quis errans ac vagus sectabitur
> rectem relinquens tramitem
> scrobis latentis pronus in foveam ruet,
> quam fodit hostilis manus,

> manus latronum, quae viantes obsidet
>   iter sequentes devium. . . .
> statum lacessunt omnipollentis Dei
>   calumniosis litibus,
> fidem minutis dissecant ambagibus
>   ut quisque lingua est nequior;
> solvant ligantque quaestionum vincula
>   per syllogismos plectiles.
>
>   (*Apoth. praef.* 1–16, 19–24)

Are we following the right path? Master, I ask you. Are we preserving the correct faith? Or have we been careless about the serpent's teachings, and slipped unknowingly? It is hard to find the straight and narrow path of salvation in the midst of twistings and turnings. Too many crossroads leap up in front of us, worn smooth by the elaborate wanderings of the faithless; slanting sideroads weave themselves together on every side. If a man, roaming erratically, follows one of them, leaving the right path, he will fall headlong into an ambush—a hidden pit dug by a band of hostile highwaymen who attack travellers following the wrong path. . . . They tear at the existence of almighty God with their slanderous arguments; they shred the faith with their twisted casuistries as well as their worthless language will allow; they knit and unravel chains of argument with their woven syllogisms.

The man searching for the correct faith is like a man wandering along a road full of twisting sideroads and confusing intersections, where he may be ambushed by the robbers (*latronum*) who prey on those who are lost on the wrong path.[24] The robbers in the poem are heretics who quarrel over the nature of God, shredding the faith into tiny pieces with their *ambagibus*, their "twisted casuistries." Like Discordia, they are weavers as well as unbinders: *solvant ligantque quaestionum vincula/per syllogismos plectiles,* "they knit and unravel chains of argument with their woven syllogisms." Binding and loosing, as in the *Psychomachia* passage we discussed in the first chapter,

[24]For the harsh reality behind this imagery, see B. D. Shaw, "Bandits in the Roman Empire," *Past and Present* 105 (1984):3–52.

have no fixed moral value in Prudentius' work. Here weaving is associated with treachery and deceit, while dissolution, which is first associated with discord, when the heretics tear the faith into pieces, is associated several lines later with correct dogma:

> nodos tenaces recta rumpit regula
> infesta dissertantibus.
> (*Apoth. praef.* 27–28)

The right rule, enemy of speakers, bursts through their tight knots.

Recta regula, the "right rule," here bursts through the rigid knots tied by the heretics; again as in the *Psychomachia,* the force of *discordia* (heresy) is conquered only when its enemy adopts its characteristics.

The description in *Peristephanon* 11 of Hippolytus' tomb on the Via Tiburtina is, like the highway of life in the *Apotheosis,* characterized by twistings, turnings, and confusion—a fit resting place for a saint who has confessed to being an *auctor erroris.* The imagery of twisting and turning is especially appropriate here, for the tomb is located in a catacomb:

> huius in occultum gradibus via prona reflexis
>   ire per anfractus luce latente docet.
> primas namque fores summo tenus intrat hiatu
>   inlustratque dies limina vestibuli.
> inde ubi progressu facili nigrescere visa est
>   nox obscura loci per specus ambiguum,
> occurrunt celsis immissa foramina tectis,
>   quae iaciant claros antra super radios.
> quamlibet ancipites texant hinc inde recessus,
>   arta sub umbrosis atria porticibus,
> at tamen excisi subter cava viscera montis
>   crebra terebrato fornice lux penetrat.
> sic datur absentis per subterranea solis
>   cernere fulgorem luminibusque frui.
> (*Perist.* 11.155–168)

Into its secret depths a path leads downward with twisting steps, showing the way in the hidden light through the maze-like turns. The light enters through the doors to the very top of the cave, and daylight shines on the threshhold of the entrance. From there the way is easy, but the remote night of the place seems to blacken and penetrate the ambiguous cavern. There are holes let into the high roof which cast bright arrows of light above the cave. Corridors weave a random pattern in the rock of narrow galleries and shaded porticoes, but even here, in the hollow bowels of the carved mountain, light crowds in through the pierced vault. Thus it is granted to the world below to see the flashing of an absent sun and enjoy its light.

The winding steps (*gradibus . . . reflexis*), the *anfractus,* the corridors (*ancipites . . . recessus*), and the weaving imagery (*texant*) combine to suggest not only the highway of life in the *Apotheosis,* but another place of confusion associated with the myth of Theseus and his son—the Cretan labyrinth, described thus by Vergil in *Aeneid* 5:

> ut quondam Creta fertur Labyrinthus in alta
> parietibus *textum* caecis iter *ancipitemque*
> mille viis habuisse dolum, qua signa sequendi
> falleret indeprensus et inremeabile error.
>   (*Aen.* 5.588–591)

> Once long ago, so they say, the Labyrinth deep below high Crete
> had a path woven from blind walls—an ambiguous trick with a
> thousand ways, insoluble, untraceable, whose clues would lead
> to hopeless confusion and wandering.

Much has been written about the significance of the labyrinth in the *Aeneid,* particularly about its appearance on the temple doors at Cumae at the opening of *Aeneid* 6. Here we may only pause to note two points that are relevant to Prudentius' adoption of the image. First, as Michael Putnam points out, the labyrinth is the product of the archetypal craftsman Daedalus and signifies a certain kind of creativity, "an inventiveness which articulates subterfuge and doubleness."[25] As such, it represents an art that is characterized by metamorphosis and hybridization, two concepts central to Prudentius' treatment of Hippolytus. Second, as William Fitzgerald has described in a recent article, the labyrinth functions as a narrative device with a dissolving frame. The labyrinthine frieze Aeneas sees on the gates at Cumae marks "the unfolding of a process by which the past is first frozen and then reintegrated into history; this is reflected in the difference between the way it breaks into the story of Aeneas and the way it leads back as the frame of art dissolves."[26] Although Prudentius never uses the word *labyrinthus* in the poem, the combination of a hero named Hippolytus, whose name suggests the Cretan legend, the confusing corridors of the underground tomb, and the painting on the wall with the ambiguous message and the dissolving frame, suggests that Prudentius had Vergil's paradigmatic ecphrasis in mind as he wrote.

The maze-like aspects of Hippolytus' tomb resemble not only the labyrinth but also Hades. Its strange illumination (*Perist.* 11.153–156, 159–160), its cavernous darkness (157–158), and its easy access (157) are stock characteristics of poetic descriptions of Hades. In Vergil's account, for example, we find the Sibyl warning Aeneas that while the descent to the underworld is easy, the return is not:

> . . . *facilis* descensus Averno:
> noctes atque dies patet atria ianua Ditis;
> sed revocare gradum superasque evadere ad auras,
> hoc opus, hic labor est.
>
> > (*Aen.* 6.126–128)

The descent to Avernus is easy. Night and day the royal gates to Hell lie open, but to retrace your steps and escape again into the upper air—this is the task, this the labor.

[25]Michael C. J. Putnam, "Daedalus, Virgil, and the End of Art," *AJPh* 108 (1987):178.

[26]William Fitzgerald, "Aeneas, Daedalus and the Labyrinth," *Arethusa* 17 (1984):57.

The strange light of the underworld is described in the *Aeneid* by a simile comparing it to the light on a road through the woods on a night when clouds block the moon:

> ibant *obscuri* sola sub *nocte* per *umbram*
> perque domos Ditis vacuas et inania regna,
> quale per *incertam lunam* sub *luce maligna*
> est iter in silvis, ubi caelum condidit umbra
> Iuppiter, et rebus nox abstulit atra colorem.
>
> (Aen. 6.268–272)

> They moved along in darkness under the lonely night, through shadow and through Hell's empty houses and vacant realms, like travelers who journey through a wood in the baleful light of an uncertain moon, when Jupiter veils the sky in shadow and black night steals all color from the world.

We find the same elements, ease of access and strange illumination, in another account of descent to the underworld, this time Theseus' description of his journey to Hades in Seneca's *Hercules Furens*. It is no trouble to go to the underworld, says Theseus, the road itself leads you: *nec ire labor est: ipsa deducit via*. His description of the underworld is similar to Prudentius' description of the odd system of reflected light in Hippolytus' tomb and is probably Prudentius' source. Here are the two passages:

> non caeca tenebris incipit primo via
> tenuis relictae lucis a tergo nitor
> fulgorque dubius solis adflicti cadit
> et ludit aciem: nocte sic mixta solet
> praebere lumen primus aut serus dies.
>
> (Hercules Furens 668–672)

At first the dark road is not entirely blinded with shadows. A faint glimmer of the light left behind, the doubtful gleam of a stricken sun, falls upon it and tricks the eye: night mixed with day, like the twilight before dawn or after sunset.

inde ubi progressu facili nigrescere visa est
  nox obscura loci, per specus ambiguum.
occurrunt celsis inmissa foramina tectis
  quae iaciant claros antra super radios . . . .
sic datur absentis per subterranea solis
  cernere fulgorem luminibusque frui.
                    (*Perist.* 11.159–162, 167–168)

From there the way is easy, but the remote night of the place
seems to blacken and penetrate the ambiguous cavern. There
are holes let into the high roof which cast bright arrows of light
into the cave. . . . Thus it is granted to the world below to see the
flashing of an absent sun.

The underworld darkness in both of these passages is partially
illuminated by a dubious half-light—the light in Seneca's
underworld is not to be trusted; the doubtful gleam of his
stricken sun deceives the eye (*ludit aciem*). In Hippolytus'
tomb, light is provided by an absent sun, but the light does not
seem greatly to illuminate the remote night, *nox obscura,* of the
place. This is the same sort of unrevealing light we find in
Plato's allegory of the cave, where the fires placed behind the
prisoners reveal only shadows, not real things. The tomb, like
the cave, is a place of uncertainty and error, cut off from the
light of its invisible sun.

The eerie, underworld atmosphere of the catacombs struck
others as well. Jerome, recalling his frequent Sunday visits to
the catacombs during his stay in Rome, describes the strange
lighting of the tombs in terms similar to the ones Prudentius
uses and is reminded of a line from *Aeneid* 2:

Dum essem Romae puer, et liberalibus studiis erudirer, sol-
ebam . . . diebus Dominicis sepulcra apostolorum et martyrum
ciruire; crebroque cryptas ingredi, quae in terrarum profunda
defossae, ex utraque parte ingredientem per parietes habent
corpora sepultorum et ita obscura sunt omnia, ut propemodum
illud propheticum compleatur: Descendant ad infernum vi-
ventes: et raro desuper lumen admissum, horrorem temperet
tenebrarum, ut non tam fenestram, quam foramen demissi lu-

minis putes: rursumque pedetentim acceditur, et caeca nocte circumdatis illud Virgilianum proponitur: Horror ubique animo, simul ipsa silentia terrent.

When I was a boy at Rome and was being educated in liberal studies, I was accustomed . . . to visit on Sundays the sepulchres of the apostles and martyrs. And often did I enter the crypts, deep dug in the earth, with their walls on either side lined with the bodies of the dead, where everything is so dark that it almost seems as if the psalmist's words were fulfilled: "Let them go down alive into hell." (Psalm 55.15) Here and there the light, not entering through windows, but filtering down from above through shafts, relieves the horror of the darkness. But again, as one cautiously moves forward, the black night closes round, and there comes to mind the line of Vergil: *horror ubique animo, simul ipsa silentia terrent* [Horror fills the mind, and at the same time the silence itself terrifies]. (Aen. 2.755)[27]

Sarah Spence, commenting on this passage, remarks: "Clearly the catacombs caught Jerome's imagination, and in a very telling way for our purposes: to him they were the repository of the darker forces of the *Aeneid*. Quoting from Book 2, at the moment when Aeneas returns to find Creusa, Jerome likens the catacombs to the outer darkness of the fall of Troy and the inner darkness of the pain and loss of a loved one."[28] Jerome's imagination was caught in a telling way for our purposes as well, for he makes an associative leap similar to the one Prudentius makes. The biblical quotation and the Vergilian quotation come to his mind simultaneously, and he does not shrink from expressing in Vergilian terms the religious thrill of horror he felt on entering the precinct of the holy dead.

Prudentius, too, finds the labyrinthine catacombs an ambiguous place where classical and Christian images overlap.

---

[27]Jerome, *Commentarius in Hiezechielem* 40 (*PL* 25, cols. 375 A-B). Translation from James Stevenson, *The Catacombs: Rediscovered Monuments of Early Christian Art* (London, 1978). Quoted in Sarah Spence, *Rhetorics of Reason and Desire: Vergil, Augustine, and the Troubadours* (Ithaca, N.Y., 1988), pp. 60–61.

[28]Spence, *Rhetorics of Reason*, p. 61.

Spence, discussing the catacomb paintings, points out that they demonstrate an analogous overlapping of systems of imagery. For although the majority of the catacomb burials are Christian, most of the paintings are of Old Testament rather than New Testament scenes. As we saw in Chapter 2, she concludes that the typological situations represented in the paintings indicate a particular relationship between the viewer and the scene depicted: the viewer is expected to interpret, by providing information not present in the painting, thus taking part in what Spence calls "the rhetoric of participation." It is fascinating, and an indication that Spence is correct in her analysis of the necessity for audience participation in the interpretation of the catacomb paintings, that Prudentius chooses to use a pagan/Christian catacomb fresco as the medium for telling the story of his hybrid saint.[29] By presenting the painting of the death of the classical Hippolytus as a focal point of his poem about the martyrdom of the new Hippolytus, he invites his audience to try to discover the implicit relationship between the two figures, the hero in the painting and the martyr who is mysteriously present in his glittering shrine at the center of the labyrinthine tomb.

The Mirror at the Center of the Labyrinth

We must return again to the relationship between the painting Prudentius claims as his inspiration for *Peristephanon* 11 and the tomb in which the fresco is supposedly painted. As I mentioned earlier in this chapter, the description of the painting is a curious ecphrasis. Prudentius begins to describe it at line 123, after his version of Hippolytus' death, and the opening of the ecphrasis is clearly marked in the text:

> Exemplar sceleris paries habet inlitus, in quo
> multicolor fucus digerit omne nefas.

[29]For a discussion of Prudentius' use of catacomb paintings in the *Cathemerinon*, see A. R. Springer, "Prudentius, Pilgrim and Poet: The Catacombs and Their Paintings as Inspiration for the *Liber Cathemerinon*," diss., University of Wisconsin at Madison, 1984.

The wall holds a painted model of the crime; many-colored paints lay bare the unspeakable.

What makes this ecphrasis curious is that it never ends—its opening is clearly signaled, but reader and poet never emerge from it, and the rest of the poem is contained within the frame of the description of the painting. Thus the description of the tomb, itself elaborately pictured, is an ecphrasis within an ecphrasis, and a number of questions are left unsolved by the text. By erasing the boundary of the ambiguous painting, Prudentius forces his readers to experience the confusion and disorientation that are emblematic of his distracted saint.

Let us examine the interior of the tomb more closely. At its center (and thus both inside the ecphrasis and outside the painting) is the silver-plated shrine containing the saint's relics:

> ipsa, illas animae exuvias quae continet intus
>   aedicula argento fulgurat ex solido.
> praefixit tabulas dives manus aequore levi
>   candentes, recavum quale nitet speculum.
>   (*Perist.* 11.183–186)

The shrine itself, which holds the sheddings of his soul, shines forth, made from solid silver. A wealthy hand covered it with smoothly polished bright tablets, which reflect like a hollow mirror.

This mirrored reliquary shrine containing the remains of the saint's body—or, as Prudentius rather oddly puts it, the "sheddings of his soul"—is a curious object. It has much in common with the painting, for it is another carefully constructed work of art that receives its own ecphrasis and, as we shall see shortly, dissolves its own frame. Furthermore, the painting and the shrine are alike in that they both, in a sense, "contain" Hippolytus: the painting holds the narrative of his death, and the shrine holds his physical remains. These two works of art with their contents which are different and yet somehow the same exemplify the repetition and hybridization

characteristic of both the labyrinth and Hippolytus. For Prudentius' Hippolytus is, unquestionably, a hybrid—the ambiguous painting, the allusions to Seneca's *Phaedra,* and the labyrinth imagery that dominates the description of the tomb
combine to force the reader to associate the martyred Hippolytus with his pagan prototype, and with the *inremeabile error*
(untraceable wandering) of the Cretan myth.

A sense of endless circularity and repetition is suggested by
the object at the center of the tomb, which both conceals and
contains Hippolytus' body. The shrine, which shines in the
ambiguous light of the tomb's absent sun, is covered with
polished metal plates that act as mirrors. Instead of revealing
its contents, the shrine reflects its surroundings, becoming a
distorted repetition of the tomb/labyrinth itself. Prudentius
signals the importance of the mirrored panels and their distorted reflection by a play on words, for the hollow mirror,
recavum speculum, which contains in its reflection the surrounding cavern, is a double anagram for cave: *cavum* and *specus* are
hidden in slightly distorted form in the phrase, so that the
words describing the hollow mirror contain in themselves another reflection of the cave.

It is typical of Prudentius that the shrine is covered with
hollow—that is, concave—mirrors, which not only reverse the
image reflected in them, but also turn it upside down. We must
marvel at the complexity of Prudentius' construction in this
passage: not only do the mirrors, in a sense, contain the entire
labyrinth that surrounds them, but the tomb itself and all its
contents are themselves contained by the painting Prudentius
describes in the open-ended ecphrasis—the painting that
forms the threshold allowing him to cross over from the world
of Christian history to the world of classical mythology.

Prudentius' Hippolytus belongs to both worlds. He is, as we
have seen, a composite figure, the focal point of a number of
closely interlocked systems of imagery linking the Christian
concepts of martyrdom and heresy to more ancient mythical
preoccupations with discord, and with doubling and repetition. In all his various incarnations, Hippolytus remains an

enigmatic figure. Half Christian and half pagan, both heretic and martyr, he is the embodiment of the paradoxical fusion of classical myth and Christianity that so distinguished the intellectual climate of the fourth century.

It is fitting that Prudentius, who seeks Hippolytus so diligently at the opening of the poem, finds him in the end in such an ambivalent space: outside the city limits, in a catacomb with all the characteristics of Hades, in a painting whose mythic subject matter becomes his source for a Christian tale of conversion and martyrdom. Prudentius' elaborate ecphrasis describing the tomb painting is important, and not simply as a piece of contemporary evidence about catacomb art. The painting, made with such carefully described skill and craftsmanship, is for the poet a mediating space, where opposing forces and ideas exist in harmony. It is, perhaps, a model for Prudentius' own art, which struggles to create a space where the mutually opposed forces of Concordia and Discordia, creation and dissolution, even Christianity and classical culture, might be able to exist in a precarious balance.[30] It is precisely at the moment when the description of the painting dissolves into the description of the mirrored shrine (lines 179–182) that Prudentius returns to speak *in propria persona,* directly to the bishop who requested the poem. He speaks as a pilgrim gazing at the reflecting mirrors of the shrine. Situating himself at the point where boundaries collapse, between a (fictional?) painting and a reflected maze where different mythologies intersect, Prudentius takes his problematic poetic stand.

[30]William Fitzgerald's reading of Vergil's treatment of the labyrinth suggests an intriguing approach to Prudentius' use of the image. In his view "it is both a highly elaborate artistic work that freezes the past in a harmlessly discontinuous relation with the present and, as an instigator of repetition that transforms pattern into path, it offers the possibility of reactivating the past and assimilating it into the flow of history" ("Aeneas, Daedalus and the Labyrinth," *Arethusa* 17 (1984):58–59).

5

Dubious Distinctions

Peristephanon 13 recounts the martyrdom of Cyprian of Carthage and his followers, known collectively as the Candida Massa. In it Prudentius explores the relationship between martyrdom, suicide, sterility, and love. He takes us through the maze he has built out of legends and literary allusions into the dark heart of Rome's ancient enemy, Carthage, showing us a saint of great and somewhat sinister seductive charm.

The Cyprian in Prudentius' poem bears little resemblance to the historical bishop and martyr. Prudentius, whether deliberately or because the traditions were already confused, has conflated Cyprian of Carthage with a character from a popular romance, Cyprian of Antioch, a magician said to have converted to Christianity.[1] The latter Cyprian, unlike the respectable bishop of Carthage, was also an accomplished seducer and dispenser of love charms, and it is this aspect of his story that particularly appeals to Prudentius, for it allows him to exploit the etymological associations of Cyprian's name.

[1]On the confusion between the two Cyprians, see T. Sabattini, "S. Cipriano nella tradizione agiografica," *Rivista di studi classici* 21 (1973):181–204; Hippolyte Delehaye, "Cyprien d'Antioche et Cyprien de Carthage," *Analecta Bollandiana* 39 (1921):314–322; T. Zahn, *Cyprian von Antiochen und die deutsche Faustsage* (Erlagen, 1882). Gregory Nazianzenus conflates the two saints in a sermon from 379, well before the writing of the *Peristephanon*, and so it is possible that the confusion was well established when Prudentius wrote the *Peristephanon*.

Cyprianus is derived from *Cypris,* one of the goddess Venus' titles, taken from her association with the island of Cyprus. We have already seen examples of Prudentius' fondness for exploiting the literal meaning of his saints' names; in this poem he signals the importance of the erotic associations of Cyprian's name by introducing the word *amor* into the text in the line following the first mention of Cyprian's name: *amore et ore nostrum* (love and language make him ours, 13.3). Combining the erotic associations of Cyprian's name with the romantic adventures of Cyprian of Antioch, Prudentius creates a character who epitomizes the seductive and sometimes violent force of eros and thus, as we shall see, is a martyr peculiarly appropriate to the city of Carthage as it appears in Roman history and literature.

The Cyprian of the *Peristephanon* is an erotic hero. In his youth he specializes in love charms and is an irresistible seducer who dissolves marriages. His physical attributes—long hair, beardless cheeks, and fair skin—are those of a stock figure in Roman erotic poetry, the beautiful but doomed youth. We will see how the figure of the doomed youth was used in earlier poetry to suggest an eros that is sterile rather than fruitful and how the earlier poets used the image of the ceremony that marks the transition from boyhood to manhood—the cutting of the lock of hair (*caesaries*). Prudentius uses the loss of the lock to symbolize Cyprian's conversion to Christianity in this poem, a spiritual conversion that is, in Cyprian's case, accompanied by a startling physical transformation from beautiful, delicate youth to bristling old man.

Cyprian is a powerful figure both before and after his conversion. His fundamental character does not change, though his appearance does. As befits his name, he is always able to inspire passionate love in others, and Prudentius characterizes this love with fiery language throughout the poem. He is also the master of a powerful kind of erotic rhetoric. Before his conversion, he seduces women with magical chants and incantations, and after it, he inspires his followers with his preaching. Indeed, his rhetoric is so important that Prudentius uses it to introduce the poem:

Punica terra tulit quo splendeat omne quidquid usquam est,
inde domo Cyprianum, sed decus orbis et magistrum.
est proprius patriae martyr, sed amore et ore noster;
incubat in Libyae sanguis, sed ubique lingua pollet,
sola superstes agit de corpore, sola obire nescit,
dum genus esse hominum Christus sinet et vigere
mundum. . . .
o nive candidius linguae genus, o novum saporem!
ut liquor ambrosius cor mitigat, imbuit palatum,
sedem animae penetrat, mentem fovet et pererrat artus,
sic Deus interius sentitur et inditur medullis.

(*Perist.* 13.1–6, 11–14)

The Punic earth bore him to make everything everywhere shine.
Cyprian's home is there, but he is the whole world's glory and
teacher. He is his own land's martyr, but love and language
[literally *ore*, mouth] make him ours; his blood broods over
Libya, but his tongue has power everywhere—his tongue, the
only survivor of his body, the only part that knows not how to
die, as long as Christ allows the race of men to live and flourish in
the world. . . . His tongue [or language, *lingua*] is whiter than
snow, a new taste! Like an ambrosial liquid, it softens the heart,
steeps the palate, penetrates the deep seat of the soul. It warms
the heart and wanders through the limbs—so god is sensed
inside, and permeates the marrow of our bones.

Prudentius' praise of Cyprian's rhetorical skills is couched in
odd language. Cyprian's *lingua,* he says, retains its ubiquitous
power long after death—not a startling sentiment if Prudentius means simply his language or rhetoric. But although the
figurative meaning of *lingua* is clearly its primary meaning in
this passage, the imagery Prudentius uses here indicates that
he wishes us to keep in mind its literal meaning as well. The
passage is saturated with language that suggests taste—Cyprian's speech is a new flavor, *novum saporem,* and is compared
to an ambrosial liquid that softens the heart and imbues the
palate. This is part of Prudentius' association of Cyprian's
rhetoric with the insidious and penetrating power of eros, but
it also reminds us of the physical process of drinking, and so,
again, of the physical meaning of *lingua.*

This is not the only peculiarity in this passage. In addition to calling the literal meaning of *lingua* to mind by the "orality" of his language, Prudentius makes the bizarre claim that Cyprian's *lingua* is the only surviving part *of his body: sed ubique lingua pollet, / sola superstes agit de corpore, sola obire nescit.* Cyprian's tongue becomes a strange, living relic in this poem. Prudentius has conflated two conventionally pious ideas—that Cyprian's language, through the power of his writing, has been able to transcend his African origins and spread through the world and that the physical remains of a martyr such as Cyprian possess tremendous power long after the saint's death— into a startling image, that of a tongue surviving its body's death.[2]

This image is, unquestionably, grotesque. And yet for those who find it difficult to believe Prudentius could or would mention, even by such an indirect method, something as unpleasant as a living but unattached tongue, we can cite a much more gruesome passage from *Peristephanon* 10, the martyrdom of another saint known for his oratory, Romanus.[3] These

---

[2]For a discussion of the power of martyr's relics, see Peter Brown's *The Cult of the Saints: Its Rise and Function in Latin Christianity* (Chicago, 1981), chaps. 4 and 5, esp. p. 78: "The relic is a detached fragment of a whole body: As Victricius said, 'You see tiny relics, a little drop of blood.' But it is precisely the detachment of the relic from its physical associations that summed up most convincingly the imaginative dialectic. . . . For how better to suppress the fact of death, than to remove part of the dead from its original context in the all too cluttered grave? How better to symbolize the abolition of time in such dead, than to add to that an indeterminacy of space? Furthermore, how better to express the paradox of the linking of Heaven and Earth than by an effect of 'inverted magnitudes,' by which the object around which boundless associations clustered would be tiny and compact?"

[3]   Aristo quidam medicus accitus venit,
proferre linguam praecipit; profert statim
martyr retectam, pandit ima et faucium.
Ille et palatum tractat et digito exitum
vocis pererrans vulneri explorat locum.

Linguam deinde longe ab ore protrahens
scalpellum in usque guttur insertans agit.
Illo secante fila sensim singula
numquam momordit martyr aut os dentibus
compressit artis, nec cruorem sorbuit.

passages are, in a sense, inversions of one another: Romanus loses his tongue, but is miraculously able to continue speaking (at great length, to the consternation of his persecuting magistrate); Cyprian's *lingua* loses Cyprian, but is still able to survive and to persuade. Prudentius dwells on the amputation of Romanus' tongue at great length (the saint himself discusses it in detail in his postsurgical speech); it is hard to imagine that he did not intend his readers to make the connection between the lost tongue of Romanus in *Peristephanon* 10 and the vigorous tongue of Cyprian in *Peristephanon* 13.

Thus Prudentius, by exploiting the incongruities of the literal and, in context, grotesque meaning of *lingua,* and its conventional figurative meaning, opens his poem by undercutting his own rhetoric—and, by extension, Cyprian's as well. For once we have entertained the notion of a disembodied tongue still preaching in the Libyan desert, we find it difficult to take Prudentius' stiffly exorbitant praise of Cyprian's rhetoric at face value. One might say that this is an overreading of the text and that Prudentius was carried away by his own imagery, but, as I shall argue, this is not the only place in the poem where the value of Cyprian's persuasive speech is undermined. *Peristephanon* 13 is, surprising as it may seem at first glance, a subtle but sustained critique not only of

> Immotus et patente rictu constitit,
> dum sanguis extra defluit scaturriens;
> perfusa pulcher menta russo stemmate
> fert, et cruenti pectoris spectat decus,
> fruiturque et ostro vestis ut iam regiae.
> (*Perist.* 10.896–910)

A certain Aristo, a doctor, comes when summoned. He orders [Romanus] to put out his tongue, and at once the martyr sticks it out as far as possible, revealing the depths of his throat. The doctor feels his palate, and letting his finger wander through the place where the voice comes out, he explores the site of the wound. Then, drawing the tongue far out from the mouth, he inserts the scalpel, driving it in as far as the throat. As he cut the strings one by one, the martyr never bit down, or clenched his teeth and closed his mouth, or swallowed the blood. Motionless, he took his stand, jaws gaping as the blood flowed and gushed out—a beautiful sight, as he lifts his chin stained with a red garland and observes the glory of his bloodied breast, enjoying it as if it were the crimson of a king's robe.

Cyprian, but of what Prudentius sees as a dangerous tendency inherent in the cult of the martyrs to equate martyrdom with self-annihilation and suicide.

Prudentius' description of Cyprian's eloquent tongue is another twist on the trope we glanced at briefly (Chapter 2) in the passage from Vergil describing the amputation of Larides' hand, which survives for a time and searches for its body. The amputation motif, very common in Roman literature, seems to appear at moments of confusion in the text.[4] It serves as a marker, pointing to the dissolution of boundaries, the restrictions that limit the individual but that also, by differentiating him from all else, determine his nature and allow him to exist at all. Most mysterious of these boundaries, and the one Vergil was most concerned with, is the *discrimen mortis,* the distinction between life and death, or matter and soul. The motif of the living limb separated from a dead or dying body graphically illustrates the crossing of the threshold that separates death from life, animate from inanimate.

Cyprian's tongue belongs in this tradition, though it seems to serve another function as well by pointing to a paradox basic to the cult of the martyrs: the martyr is both dead and alive, present in his relics yet absent in heaven. Peter Brown describes how, through the reading of the saint's passion (*passio*) in his shrine, categories apparently distinct could appear to be reconciled through the presence (*praesentia*) of the martyr:

So the *passio* brought the past into the present. Coinciding as it did with the high point of the saint's festival, the reading of the

---

[4]There are many examples of the survival of amputated body parts in Latin literature: Philomela's tongue, which wriggles along the ground searching for its mistress, and Orpheus' head, which sings as it floats down the Hebrus, are two notorious examples from Ovid's *Metamorphoses* (6.549–560 and 11.50–53, respectively). See also Lucretius' description (*DRN* 3.642–656) of soldiers cut down in battle whose severed limbs continue to fight; Lucan's *Pharsalia* 1.377–378, in which a hand has a mind of its own; and another vignette from Ovid *Met.* 5.99–106, in which the head of an old man named Emathion continues to speak after it has been cut off.

passio gave a vivid, momentary face to the invisible *praesentia* of the saint. When the *passio* was read, the saint was "really" there: a sweet scent filled the basilica, the blind, the crippled, and the possessed began to shout that they now felt his power in healing, and those who had offended him in the past had good reason to tremble.[5]

In the martyr's shrine, past and present coalesce; the power of the absent saint is made manifest in the frailest of those present, and the corruption and stench of death are replaced by a sweet scent that issues from the tomb of the saint and fills the basilica.

This dizzying conjunction of opposites inherent in the cult of the martyrs fascinates Prudentius, a poet who, as we saw in the *Psychomachia*, is enthralled by polarities. In *Peristephanon* 13 he examines some of the contradictory forces at play in the processes of conversion and martyrdom. Everything about Prudentius' hero is paradoxical. Even in the opening lines of the poem, he appears to occupy mutually exclusive categories. Cyprian is Punic by birth, but he has illuminated everything everywhere; his home is in Africa, but his glory and teaching belong to the world. His martyrdom makes him African, but he is ours (presumably Roman) because of his passion (*amor*) and his speech. The word Prudentius uses here, *ore,* could refer to his rhetoric, which is universal, to the language in which he wrote (which was Latin) or, most literally, to his lips or mouth. He seems to transcend all attempts to characterize him.

As the poem progresses, Cyprian's double nature becomes more apparent. On the most basic level, Prudentius' Cyprian is more than the Cyprian he appears to be: he is not only Cyprian of Carthage, but Cyprian of Antioch as well, for Prudentius has conflated the two saints' legends, giving the Carthaginian bishop a lurid past and a dramatic conversion.

[5]Peter Brown, *The Cult of the Saints: Its Rise and Function in Latin Christianity* (Chicago, 1981), p. 82.

Sterile Eros

Before his conversion, Cyprian has the standard attributes of the beautiful youth—long, flowing hair, smooth, beardless skin, and a beautiful face. His conversion, which happens abruptly in the poem, affects him as the end of boyhood would: the translucent beauty of his skin fades, his smooth skin grows rough, and he cuts his hair.

In Horace's ode 4.10, the narrator watches the lovely boy Ligurinus and predicts the unhappy moment when Ligurinus will become a man:

> O crudelis adhuc et Veneris muneribus potens,
> insperata tuae cum veniet pluma superbiae
> et, quae nunc umeris involitant, decederint comae
> nunc et qui color est puniceae flore prior rosae
> mutatus, Ligurine, in faciem verterit hispidam:
> dices "heu" quotiens te speculo videris alterum,
> "quae mens est hodie, cur eadem non puero fuit,
> vel cur his animis incolumes non redeunt genae?"

Still cruel, still potent with Venus' favors now, when unexpected down comes upon your pride, and when the hair which tumbles down your shoulders has fallen; when the blush which now is lovelier than any crimson rose has changed, and turned your face to stubble—then, Ligurinus, whenever you stare into the mirror you will find a different self, and you will sigh and ask, "Why is my mind not the same as when I was a boy? Or now that my mind has changed, why won't my unmarked cheeks return?"

Ligurinus, like Cyprian, will lose his rosy cheeks, his beardless skin, and his long hair, and this physical change will coincide with another, more shattering one. Horace, a rejected lover, looks forward to the moment when Ligurinus' mind will be split from his body, when the cruel (*crudelis*) and relentlessly selfish boy will learn that, as his indifference to love fades, so do his chances of attaining it. Though he is presently endowed with all the gifts of Venus (*Veneris muneribus potens*), he uses his power only to refuse love. Later he will sigh into his mirror, not even, like Narcissus, captivated by his own beauty, but already lamenting its unfamiliar absence.

Statius, in *Silvae* 3.4, uses the cutting of the lock in a more pointed way.[6] He wrote the poem to celebrate the cutting of a young man's hair and the dedication of the lock to the temple of Asclepius in Pergamum. The circumstances of the commission were peculiar, however, because the young man who is the subject of the poem, Earinus, was the emperor Domitian's lover, and Domitian had had the boy castrated to preserve his youthful beauty. Thus Statius had to celebrate the rite of passage of a boy who would never attain sexual maturity. To make matters worse, or at least more embarrassing, Domitian had passed a law forbidding castration. Under the circumstances, as Juvenal said in another context, it would be difficult *not* to write satire, though, clearly, it might be dangerous to do so. Statius, walking the tightrope with typical Roman agility, manages to hide his irony behind apposite, but ambiguous, mythical allusions. He compares Earinus' hair to other famous locks and heads of hair, but the comparisons he makes all have ominous implications.

Earinus' hair is, says Statius, more beautiful than the locks of Nisus and Achilles:

> huic et purpurea cedet coma saucia Nisi
> et quam Spercheio tumidus servat Achilles.
> > (*Silvae* 3.4.84–85)

Even the wounded crimson lock of Nisus would have to yield to this one, and the lock which swollen Achilles saved for Spercheius.

In both these mythological parallels, the cutting of the hair sealed the hero's fate and became the portent of his unhappy

---

[6]Much of this discussion of *Silvae* 3.4 is a summary of John Garthwaite's excellent "Appendix: Statius' *Silvae* 3.4: On the Fate of Earinus," *ANRW* 2, no. 1 (1984):111–124.

end. This is not the only time Statius uses mythological precedent to hint that Earinus has been condemned to a bitter fate. Earlier in the poem Venus, who is enchanted with Earinus' beauty, compares him to four other beautiful youths: Endymion, Attis, Narcissus, and Hylas, whose fates epitomize the sterility of the love they inspired or endured. Endymion was cast into a perpetual slumber by the goddess of the moon; Attis was driven to a mad passion for the goddess Cybele and castrated himself; Narcissus, who rejected all lovers of both sexes, was finally trapped by his own reflection; and Hylas, the lover of Hercules, was taken beneath the waters of a pool by an impetuous nymph. As Garthwaite points out, all the characters who serve as comparisons to or models for Earinus are characterized by *sterilis amor,* "sterile love." These beautiful boys, destroyed by the dangerous transition from adolescence to manhood, perfectly fit the paradigm described by Marcel Detienne in his *Gardens of Adonis.* To summarize briefly, Detienne demonstrates that the myths connected with Adonis form part of a complex of Greek myths centered around marriage. In this paradigm, the youth who rejects sexuality entirely, such as Narcissus or Hippolytus, is the counterpart to, and shares the same fate as, the youth who indulges in premature and excessive (i.e., nonmarital) sexual potency. As Detienne says:

> The lack of maturity, sexual union before coming of age, and the sowing of sterile seed are features which all combine to create an image which is the negative of marriage and fertile sexual union, and which stress the impotence and sterility of Adonis. However, as the myth indicates, what falls short of marriage is simply the other side to what exceeds it. The other side to the sterile sowing of seed is an excessive sexual potency. . . . Violent waxing and violent waning are inseparable terms: sexual excess (*aklosia*) brings in its wake a premature old age, the inevitable consequence of a precocious adolescence.[7]

[7]Marcel Detienne, *The Gardens of Adonis,* trans. Janet Lloyd (Sussex, 1977), p. 119.

Cyprian, at the moment of his conversion to Christianity, has much in common with Earinus and Adonis. Indeed his physical transformation upon conversion is exactly what Detienne's paradigm calls for—after a youth marked by excessive sexual fervor, Cyprian leaps prematurely into old age in a moment marked by the cutting of his long, flowing hair (*caesaries*):

> luxuriae rabiem tantae cohibet repente Christus,
> discutit et tenebras de pectore, pellit et furorem,
> implet amore sui, dat credere, dat pudere facti.
> iamque figura alia est quam quae fuit oris et nitoris:
> exuitur tenui vultus cute, transit in severam,
> deflua caesaries conpescitur ad breves capillos.
>
> (*Perist.* 13.25–30)

Suddenly Christ put an end to this mad profligacy, shook the darkness from his breast, drove out his fury, filled him with love of himself, gave him faith, gave him shame for his past. And now Cyprian's face is very different from his former shining beauty: he sheds his appearance with his tender skin and becomes harsh; his flowing locks are cut back to short bristles.

The moment of conversion is sudden, *repente*, and drastic in its thoroughness. Cyprian is changed from the inside out, as Christ drives out his old self, characterized by *rabiem* (madness), *tenebras* (darkness), and *furorem* (fury), and gives him a new one defined by love, belief, and shame. Cyprian himself is entirely passive throughout this transformation. His body seems to transform itself spontaneously to match his new soul.

As we watch the conversion of Cyprian, we see the creation of a new man, but it is a rebirth that takes place through a series of losses: the loss of beauty, the loss of the *caesaries*, that symbol of young masculinity, and the loss, literally, of face. Cyprian, strangely reversing the annual ritual of the snake, sheds the smooth shining skin of his youth for the rougher coat of ascetic maturity: *exuitur tenui vultus cute, transit in severam (Perist.* 13.29). The suggestion of snake imagery recalls another sexually ambiguous figure, the Theban seer Tiresias, who undergoes drastic physical transformations. He is turned into a woman when he tries to separate a pair of copulating snakes, but later regains his original form. As an indirect result of his sex change, he is blinded by Juno and thus remains symbolically impotent, but in recompense for his physical disability he is given the power of prophecy.

Cyprian's sexuality, like that of Tiresias and the beautiful but doomed youths already mentioned, though expressed as indiscriminate eroticism in Prudentius' account of his misspent youth, is ultimately sterile.[8] Though his spells give him unquestionable power in the sphere of love, it is the power not of generation but of seduction and leads to nothing but the disruption of the social order, as Prudentius sums it up in line 24: *quo geniale tori ius solverat aestuante nupta.* Cyprian's erotic power, characterized here as elsewhere in the poem by the element fire (*aestuante nupta,* "he sets the bride aflame"), results only in the destruction of the *geniale tori ius,* "the bond of generation" epitomized by the marriage bed.

After his conversion, Cyprian becomes a new man, a man defined by loss, whose most burning wish is for martyrdom. But, paradoxically, though Cyprian changes his appearance and his religion, though he abandons the sensual life and becomes an ascetic and a bishop of the church, he does not change his name, and it is his name that reveals the part of his character untouched by his conversion. Cyprian's name marks him as a man under the sway of Venus and set apart from the most fundamental social institution, marriage. His seductive powers are, as we shall see, redirected but not basically changed by either his physical or his mental transformation.

Prudentius' portrayal of Cyprian as an Adonis-like sterile seducer, in accordance with the etymology of his name, which

[8]Detienne, *Gardens of Adonis,* pp. 102–105, has a fascinating discussion of the many connections between seduction and sterility in the Adonis myth. The same complex of associations (excessive heat, seduction, impotence, and sterility) that characterize ancient treatments of the Adonis myth are present in Roman poetic treatments of *sterilis amor.*

associates him with Venus, is appropriate for the poem's setting as well. The city of Carthage plays a significant role in
Prudentius' conception of Cyprian's character. For, as it turns
out, there were compelling reasons, both literary and historical, for Prudentius to associate Carthage with love and death,
martyrdom and suicide, and it is to this aspect of the poem that
we turn next.

City of Darkness

At the opening of *Peristephanon* 13, Prudentius emphatically
reminds us that Cyprian is a Carthaginian saint. In each of the
first three lines, he stresses Cyprian's African origins and then
makes a counter-claim to show that he belongs to the rest of
the world as well. While it is common for those writing in
praise of the martyrs to begin with a reference to the place of
martyrdom, the triple reference to Carthage seems to put an
unnatural stress upon the city and forces us to see Cyprian as a
primarily *Punic* or African hero.

Africa in Prudentius' day was, to borrow a phrase from Peter
Brown, a "stagnant and affluent backwater."[9] An extremely
wealthy agricultural province, its population was sharply divided between the Latin-speaking landowning class, with its
Roman culture, and the Punic-speaking peasants. It was also
the home of the Donatist movement, one of the most dangerous challenges to the post-Constantinian alliance of church
and state in the Late Antique period. The Donatists, like so
many heretical groups, wished to separate the church from the
world and to preserve its purity and holiness. This urge to see
the church as an untouched safe haven completely separate
from and opposed to sinful human life was shared by the
African Catholics as well. As Brown says,

> The Africans' view of the church had depended on their being
> able to see in it a group different from the "world," an alterna-

<hr />

[9]Brown, *Augustine of Hippo* (Berkeley and Los Angeles, 1967), p. 24.

tive to something "unclean" and hostile. The spread of Christianity in Africa, by indiscriminately filling the churches, had simply washed away the clear moral landmarks that separated the "church" from the "world." In the conditions of the third century, S. Cyprian could well expect his convert or his penitent to find himself "among the saints"; Augustine knew only too well that he was just as likely to rub shoulders with the most notorious landgrabber of the neighbourhood.[10]

The Donatists and the Catholics differed in their conceptions of who should make up the church. The Donatists rigidly excluded sinners, most particularly unworthy bishops; they opposed themselves to the society around them. The Catholics, now firmly allied with the government of the empire, saw the church as a body working through and in history, with a mission to dominate the Roman world. The differences between the two beliefs about the nature of the church originated, or at least crystallized, in 311, over the question of whom to appoint as bishop of Carthage. Caecilian, the Catholic bishop at the time, was thought to have been appointed by a *traditor,* a backsliding bishop who had failed to uphold the faith during the persecution of Diocletian. This, in the eyes of certain bishops, made Caecilian's ordination invalid; they held a council and appointed a new bishop in his place, a man quickly succeeded by Donatus, who gave the Donatist movement its name.

This was only the beginning of a long and violent schism in the African church. For Donatism, though it seems to be a religion of minority appeal, in fact was the religion of the majority in Northern Africa, a relatively closed and isolated society set off, at least in its own eyes, from the rest of the world. And the Donatists were fiercely aggressive in their pursuit of purity:

Anyone who reads a Donatist pamphlet, or, indeed, a work of S. Cyprian, will be struck by the power of the idea of ritual purity

[10]Brown, *Augustine,* p. 213.

that stemmed straight from the Old Testament: the fear of a sudden loss of spiritual potency through contact with an "unclean" thing, and the elemental imagery of the "good" and the "bad" water. Such ideas had lost little of their force in fourth century Africa. Even the sophisticated Roman still regarded religion as a precise code of rites, designed to establish the correct relationship of the community to its God (or gods). . . . The Donatist enthusiasts carried clubs called "Israels"; they would "purify" Catholic basilicas with coats of whitewash; they would destroy the altars of others. Such men could understand, far better perhaps than Augustine with his sophisticated, "spiritual" exegesis of the Old Testament, the urgent need for "separation," for the active, physical destruction of the "unclean," that runs as a constant refrain through the pages of the Bible.[11]

On the extreme fringes of the Donatist movement were the roving bands of holy men and women known as Circumcellions. These people were particularly devoted to the cult of the martyrs and lived their lives in perpetual pilgrimage from one whitewashed shrine to another; their chief aim was to suffer a martyr's death themselves. They were known for their atrocities: attacks on Catholic bishops and wealthy landowners, attacks on Catholic churches, and suicide in the pursuit of martyrdom.[12]

To the Donatists, the church was and ought to remain the church of the martyrs, and the martyr to whom they claimed the strictest adherence was their own countryman, Cyprian.[13] Their rigid theology was based on the doctrine of the church

[11]Brown, *Augustine*, pp. 218–219.

[12]For Augustine's attitude toward the Donatist movement, see Brown, *Augustine*, pp. 212–243. For comments on the atrocities committed by the Circumcellions, see Augustine, *Epistulae* 135.4.15, 108.6.19, 105.2.13, and *Contra Gaudentium* 1.28.32. For a bibliography on the Circumcellions, see Yves Congar, *Traités Anti-Donatistes* vol. 1 (Paris, 1963), pp. 32–37 and 128–130. The best book on Donatism remains W. H. C. Frend's *The Donatist Church: A Movement of Protest in Roman North Africa* (Oxford, 1952), but see also his article "The *Cellae* of the African Circumcellions," *JTS* n.s. 3 (1952): 87–89.

[13]See Jean-Paul Brisson, *Autonomisme et Christianisme dans l'Afrique romaine de Septime Sévère à l'invasion vandale* (Paris, 1958), pp. 138–153, 178–187.

in Cyprian's time, and they adopted his teachings on the sacraments and on the complete separation of the church from the world.[14] But Cyprian, though the Donatists' primary saint, was not primarily a Donatist saint: the African Catholics, particularly Augustine, claimed to follow his teachings as well. Both sides looked on Cyprian as the central figure in the early African church; both sides claimed his authority to justify their own positions. Thus the schism in the church was, in a sense, projected back onto its patron saint, as each side claimed Cyprian as its spiritual father. Given this duality in the African church, it is not surprising that Prudentius presents Cyprian as a paradoxical figure, one whose relationship to his native land is highly ambivalent, one whose advocacy of martyrdom was, given the Catholic attitude toward the Donatists and their false martyrdoms, somewhat suspect.

If Prudentius wished to portray Carthage as a dangerous place because of its associations with the schism in the African church, he had ample supporting material at hand in the descriptions of Carthage in the classical poetic tradition. Carthage in *Peristephanon* 13 appears much like the Carthage of the *Aeneid* and Silius' *Punica*, Rome's old enemy and its mirror image. (Though Prudentius was not to know it, the ultimate irony in the long rivalry between the two cities was that when Rome was sacked in 408, many prominent Romans took refuge in Carthage.) To readers brought up on the legend of Carthage—the city of Dido and of Hannibal and the city whose defeat, in the eyes of Roman writers from Sallust to Silius, marked simultaneously Rome's greatest moment and the beginning of her decline into a corrupt and corrupting empire—the appearance of an emphatically Punic hero such as Cyprian likely had unfavorable connotations. Prudentius, rather than ignoring the traditional associations of Carthage, chooses instead to emphasize them. His hero is a hybrid figure, a master of Roman eloquence sprung from the sands of Libya, and this ambivalence about the affiliations of the saint

[14]Frend, "Heresy and Schism as Social and National Movements," in *Religion Popular and Unpopular in the Early Christian Centuries* (London, 1976), p. 44.

himself reflects a deeper polarization at the heart of the poem, which is brought out by the characterization of Cyprian as an erotic figure. Cyprian's power is the power of *amor,* and Carthage, as we are about to see, is associated, both in the *Aeneid* and the *Punica,* with the madness of love.

At the beginning of the poem Prudentius suggests, but does not make explicit, the negative aspects of Carthage. The poet's rhetoric, which places Africa in opposition to the rest of the world, reminds us of the image of Carthage as Rome's enemy without recalling it directly. Later in the poem the city appears in an unflattering light in a brief passage that recalls the Carthage of Vergil and Silius:

> his ubi corda virum Christo calefacta praeparavit,
> ducitur ante alios proconsule perfurente vinctus.
> antra latent Tyriae Carthaginis abditis reposta,
> conscia Tartareae caliginis, abdicata soli.
>
> (Perist. 13.49–52)

When he had heated men's hearts and prepared them for Christ, he was bound by the raging proconsul and led ahead of the others. Caves lie deep in the hidden parts of Tyrian Carthage, caves hidden from the sun, which know the gloom of Tartarus.

In the last two lines of the passage, the insistent repetition of sounds (*Tyriae Carthaginis abditis; Tartareae caliginis abdicata*) hints at an underlying similarity in sense as well as in sound between Tyrian Carthage and the gloomy pit of Tartarus— Cyprian's cavernous prison is, in a sense, an entrance to the underworld.

Prudentius is by no means the first poet to make this association. Silius Italicus, in his description of the temple of Dido in *Punica* 1, stresses the infernal and supernatural aspects of the site:

> urbe fuit media sacrum genetricis Elissae
> manibus et patria Tyriis formidine cultum,
> quod taxi circum et piceae squalentibus umbris

abdiderant caelique arcebant lumine, templum.
hoc sese, ut perhibent, curis mortalibus olim
exuerat regina loco. stant marmore maesto
effigies, Belusque parens omnisque nepotum
a Belo series; stat gloria gentis Agenor,
et qui longa dedit terris cognomina Phoenix.
ipsa sedet tandem aeternum coniuncta Sychaeo;
ante pedes ensis Phrygius iacet; ordine centum
stant arae caelique deis Erebique potenti.
hic, crine effuso, atque Hennaeae numina divae
atque Acheronta vocat Stygia cum veste sacerdos.
immugit tellus rumpitque horrenda per umbras
sibila, inaccensi flagrant altaribus ignes.
tum magico volitant cantu per inania manes
exciti, vultusque in marmore sudat Elissae.

(Punica 1.81–98)

In the middle of the city stood a temple sacred to the ghost of
Elissa, mother of Carthage, worshipped with ancestral fear by
the Tyrians. Yew trees and pines hid it with their ragged shadows and protected it from the light of heaven. This was the
place, so they say, where the queen long ago shed her mortal
cares. Sad stone statues stand there: Belus the father and the
whole line of his descendants. Agenor, glory of his people,
stands there, and Phoenix, who gave an enduring name to his
land. Dido herself sits, joined to Sychaeus for eternity; at her feet
lies the Trojan sword; a hundred altars stand in order to the
gods of the sky and the ruler of hell. Here the priestess with
streaming hair and a Stygian robe calls on the powers of Per-
sephone and Acheron. The ground bellows; horrible sibilant
hisses shatter the shadows; fires flare on unlit altars. Then the
dead, awakened by the magic song, fly through empty space,
and Elissa's face sweats inside its marble.

Here, in the center of the city, shrouded in darkness and
hidden from the light of the sun, is Dido's temple, sacred to
the powers of the underworld and a locus for sorcery and
necromancy. The temple stands, as Silius tells us, on the very
spot where Dido killed herself. He uses two passages from the

Aeneid as the basis for his description: the first is *Aeneid* 1.440–445, a description of Dido's temple to Juno, and the second is *Aeneid* 4.504–516, a description of Dido's funeral pyre, which has many of the same details as the passage from the *Punica:*

> at regina pyra penetrali in sede sub auras
> erecta ingenti taedis atque ilice secta,
> intenditque locum sertis et fronde coronat
> funerea; super exuvias ensemque relictum
> effigiemque toro locat haud ignara futuri.
> stant arae circum et crinis effusa sacerdos
> ter centum tonat ore deos, Erebumque Chaosque
> tergeminamque Hecaten, tria virginis ora Dianae.
> sparserat et latices simulatos fontis Averni
> falcibus et messae ad lunam quaeruntur aenis
> pubentes herbae nigri cum lacte veneni;
> quaeritur et nascentis equi de fronte revulsus
> et matri praeruptus amor.
>
> (*Aen.* 4.504–516)

But when the queen has erected a pyre under the sky in the courtyard deep within the house and built it up with pine logs and hewn ilex, she fixes garlands around the place and crowns it with a funeral branch. Knowing the future all too well, she places his remains, his cast-off sword, and his effigy on the bed. Altars stand all around and a priestess with streaming hair calls in a thundering voice upon three hundred gods, upon Erebus and Chaos and triple-formed Hecate, and the three forms of the virgin Diana. And she sprinkled waters she pretended to have drawn from the fountains of Avernus, and she seeks herbs cut with a bronze sickle by moonlight and flowing with black, venomous milk; and she seeks the love-token torn from the brow of a just-born colt before the mother could steal it.

Here, too, Dido's funeral pyre is associated with necromancy: Aeneas' image is placed upon the couch; there are altars set up to the gods of the underworld; there is a priestess with loosened hair and all the ingredients necessary to cast a magic spell. Dido builds her pyre under the pretext of casting a spell

that will either bring Aeneas back to her or free her forever of
her love for him (*Aen.* 4.479). In the *Punica,* the association
with magic remains, but the love charm is replaced by spells to
raise the dead (*Pun.* 1.97–98).

In the epic tradition, Carthage is at the center of a world of
erotic magic, fatal love, necromancy, and (as we will see) human sacrifice. Prudentius, when he equates Cyprian's prison
with the caverns of the underworld, nods to that tradition; he
has already established Cyprian's place in it by presenting him
as a converted sorcerer and seducer, details that do not belong
in the sober, well-documented account of the martyrdom of
Cyprian of Carthage. Like Gregory Nazianzenus, Prudentius
may have simply confused the two Cyprians, but the erotic and
magical elements he borrowed from the story of Cyprian of
Antioch enable him, wittingly or unwittingly, to place his
saint within the poetic tradition associated with Dido and her
doomed city, and so to move from the world of Christian
history to the world of myth.

The Dido legend, particularly its treatment in epic, provided Prudentius with a tradition in which Carthage appears
as a city whose roots, like the roots of the famous oak tree in
the simile in *Aeneid* 4, reach into the underworld. In both the
Punica and the *Aeneid,* Carthage's heart of darkness is given a
physical location. In the *Aeneid,* it is Dido's funeral pyre, hidden in the innermost recesses of the palace; in the *Punica,* it is
the site of her suicide, upon which a magnificent but somber
temple has been erected. In the eyes of the Carthaginians,
Dido's pyre is the site not of her death but of her apotheosis, a
version of the story which conflicts with her definitive position
in Roman literature as a ghost in the underworld. Silius, echo-
ing a passage from *Aeneid* 1, associates the site of Dido's pyre
with Vergil's description of the temple of Juno and thus with
the place where the Phoenicians found the horse's head buried in the ground, Juno's sign to them that they had found the
spot to begin the construction of their city. The site of the
temple/pyre is thus a topological representation of the para-
doxes of the Dido story. On the one hand, it marks the origin

of the city and the apotheosis of its founder; on the other hand, it marks the site of Dido's miserable suicide and foreshadows the destruction she brought upon her city by her oath of eternal enmity with the descendants of Aeneas.

So Dido's temple, as it appears in Vergil and Silius, marks a spot where love, suicide, and self-sacrifice converge. It is not the only temple of sinister aspect in Carthage, however. There is also the temple of Kronos-Baal, where the Carthaginians carried out their notorious practice of child-sacrifice.[15] In times of grave crisis, they would sacrifice the children of prominent citizens and throw their bodies into a fiery pit—a custom Silius dramatizes in a memorable scene of the *Punica*, in which the leaders of Carthage decide to sacrifice the son of the absent Hannibal. At the beginning of the scene, moreover, Silius goes out of his way to associate the custom with Dido:

> mos fuit in populis, quod condidit advena Dido,
> poscere caede deos veniam, ac flagrantibus aris
> (infandum dictu!) parvos imponere natos.
>
> *(Pun. 4.765–767)*

> It was the custom among the people founded by the newcomer, Dido, to demand pardon from the gods with slaughter and (unspeakable to say!) to immolate tiny children on flaming altars.[16]

[15]How widespread this practice was in the Roman period is the subject of much debate. See Aline Rousselle's discussion in *Porneia: On Desire and the Body in Antiquity* (Oxford, 1988), pp. 107–128; P.-A. Février and R. Guéry, "Les Rites funéraires de la Nécropole de Sétif," *Antiquités Africaines* 15 (1980):91–124; Marcel Leglay, *Saturne Africain: Histoire* (Paris, 1966); Claude Lepelley, "Iuvenes et Circoncellions: Les derniers sacrifices humains de l'Afrique antique," *Antiquités Africaines* 15 (1980):261–272.

[16]I am unable to reproduce Silius' gruesome (and yet flippant) pun in English: *INFANdum dictu*). For more on human sacrifice in Carthage, see Marcel Leglay, *Saturne Africain: Historie* (Paris, 1966), esp. pp. 311–337, in which he discusses ritual sacrifice. He quotes all the ancient sources who mention infant sacrifice in Carthage (pp. 314–327). See also J. Teixidor, *The Pagan God* (Princeton, N.J., 1977), chaps. 1 and 2, for Phoenician and Semitic gods in the Graeco-Roman Near East.

With this background in place, we begin to see the complex-
ities of Prudentius' poem. Carthage, Dido's city, is indeed an
appropriate setting for a poem in which the poet scrutinizes
the impulses behind the passion for martyrdom. The Carthaginian setting casts the martyrdom of Cyprian and his followers into doubt, for it associates them with erotic madness,
suicide, and human sacrifice. Prudentius adopts the Roman
epic view of Carthage—that is, Carthage appears as a threat to
Rome but is also its mirror image. This notion may be based on
another etymological and anagrammatical wordplay: Carthage, ruled by the passionate queen Dido, appears as the city
of unrestrained AMOR, while ROMA, whose destiny is con-
trolled and ensured by warfare and military power, stands
opposed to it, living up to the Greek meaning of its name
(ROMÉ, "violence" or "force").

The love that drives Cyprian and his followers to martyrdom is *religionis amor,* but is no less violent for its religious
nature. Prudentius shows the passion that inspires his erotic
saint and his followers to be a kind of madness, leading not to
oneness with God, but to self-destruction and sterility. In the
next section we shall see how Prudentius drives home this
point in his description of the martyrdom of Cyprian's followers, the Candida Massa, whose deaths in a pit filled with
burning lime are described in language that echoes Ovid's
description of the creation of the world in *Metamorphoses* 1.[17]
But Prudentius shows us a creation in reverse—the reduction
of human beings into raw matter.

Together: A New Beginning?

Cyprian's hallmark throughout the poem is his ability to
break down boundaries of all sorts with his pervasive, persua-

[17]This pit is similar to the fiery pit of Tartarus which Prudentius associates
with Cyprian's Carthaginian prison and with the fiery pit into which the
Carthaginians threw their sacrificed children, described by Diodorus Siculus
as follows: "There was in Carthage a bronze statue of Kronos, his hands

sive, erotic rhetoric. As a magician, he uses his seductive magic to break down various sorts of barriers and bonds—he destroys *pudicitia* (presumably the virginity of young girls), enters tombs (thus transgressing the boundary between the living and the dead), and dissolves the fruitful bond between husband and wife, (*Perist.* 13.21–24). At his own conversion, as we have suggested, he is caught at a moment of transition between child and adult and, snake-like, he sheds one complete self and becomes another. As his name indicates, Cyprian is an exemplar of eros, which sets aflame, penetrates, breaks down barriers, and merges things together. The unrestrained binding force Cyprian commands is similar to that of Concordia in the *Psychomachia* and opposite to the power represented by Hippolytus, who epitomizes the divisive force of Discordia. And yet, though the forces are oppositely charged, when unrestrained they bring about the same result: the destruction of the creative tension that holds things in their place. In this section we shall examine the effect of Cyprian's erotic power of persuasion on his followers and why Prudentius ends his account of Cyprian's martyrdom with a parodic example of universal collapse and chaos.

Cyprian, in 13.37–47, urges his people to join their souls to Christ and earn a martyr's death. Inspired by his words, three hundred of them rush to martyr themselves by leaping into a pit of burning lime, thus forging themselves into a single, shining mass of matter. After this glorious death, Prudentius assures us, they *deserved* to be known collectively as the Candida Massa: "*Candida Massa*" *dehinc dici meruit per omne saeclum* (line 87). Once again, Prudentius appears to be adding material that does not belong to the martyrdom of Cyprian of Carthage. The Candida Massa are attested—Augustine mentions that there were one hundred fifty-three martyrs known collectively by that name—but they are associated not with Carthage but with Utica, and there is no attestation of a form

stretched out, palms up but inclining towards the earth in such a way that the child laid on them would roll down and fall into a ditch filled with flames" (Diod. Sic. 20.14.4–6).

of death remotely like the one Prudentius describes in this poem.[18] It seems clear, then, that Prudentius has deliberately introduced this bizarre episode into Cyprian's story for his own purposes, and so it deserves a closer look.

As we read the description of the effects of Cyprian's preaching on his followers, it becomes clear that although he shed his magician's skin to become a bishop, he did not lose his magical powers of persuasion:

> . . . influebat inde
> Spiritus in populum Carthaginis, auctor acrioris
> ingenii, stimulis ut pectora subditis calerent
> ad decus egregium discrimine sanguinis petendum
> non trepidare docens nec cedere nec dolore vinci,
> laudis amore rapi, Christum sapere et fidem tueri.
>
> (*Perist.* 13.70–75)

Then the Spirit flowed into the Carthaginian people, and created a fiercer character, so that their hearts were pricked into flames, and they yearned to seek outstanding distinction at the price of their blood. He taught them not to fear, not to yield, not to be conquered by pain; to be carried away by the love of glory, to know Christ, and to guard their faith.

As at the opening of the poem, Cyprian's eloquence is ascribed to the Holy Spirit and is accompanied by water imagery (here, *influebat*, 13.70; at the opening of the poem, *fluxerat*, 13.9, and *fontibus . . . inrigavit*, 13.10). The effect of this flowing eloquence is expressed as a sort of seduction: the people's hearts grow hot under the pricks of persuasion (*stimulis ut pectora subditis calerent*, 13.72), and they learn to submit to a form of love, *laudis amore rapi* (13.75).[19] Similarly, in the beginning of the poem we find the saint's language (*lingua*) seeping into

---

[18]See Lavarenne's preface to *Perist.* 13 (*Oeuvres* [Paris 1955]), and see Augustine, *Enarr. in psalm.* 49.9 (*PL* 36 col. 571); *Serm.* 306 (*PL* 38 col. 1400–1405) (on the Candida Massa) and *Serm.* 311 (*PL* 38 col. 1417).

[19]For *stimulus* used in an erotic context, see, for example, Ovid *Fasti* 2.779 and Livy 30.14.1.

minds, softening hearts, wandering through the limbs, and generally behaving like the insidious *amor* of erotic poetry.[20] The same erotic persuasiveness characterizes both his early days as a seducer, when his magic charms enabled him to melt the resistance of brides and young girls at will, and his later rhetoric of martyrdom.

The *amor laudis* with which Cyprian inspires his congregation has its sinister counterpart elsewhere in Roman literature. In the *Aeneid*, for example, the suicidal aspect of the lust for glory is examined repeatedly, perhaps most notably in the Nisus and Euryalus episode from *Aeneid* 9.[21] For these two, love of glory and passion for one another are inextricably intertwined. Vergil opens the scene with a description of the comrades, whose love is defined by their position in battle—*his amor unus erat, pariterque in bella ruebat,* one love united them, and together they rushed into battle (*Aen.* 9.182). Nisus, in the opening words of his speech announcing his plans for a dangerous night mission through the enemy camp, recognizes the danger of his desire for martial glory, but finds its compulsion irresistible. He wonders about the source of such a powerful desire, and his question sets the tone for the rest of the episode:

> Nisus ait: "dine hunc ardorem mentibus addunt,
> Euryale, an sua cuique deus fit dira cupido?"
> (*Aen.* 9.184–185)

> Nisus said, "Do the gods set this burning in our minds, Euryalus, or does fatal desire become a god for each of us?"

Euryalus has no answer, but as he listens to the scheme he is struck by the same deadly desire: *obstipuit magno laudum percussus amore* (*Aen.* 9.197).

---

[20] . . . *ut liquor ambrosius cor mitigat, inbuit palatum / sedem animae penetrat, mentem fovet et pererrat artus,* 13.12–13 (Like an ambrosial liquid, it softens the heart, steeps the palate, penetrates the deep seat of the soul. It warms the heart and wanders through the limbs . . .).

[21] But compare also *Aen.* 5.229ff., 6.819–823, 6.889, 7.496, 10.449ff.

This love of glory, of the *kleos* that sets the hero apart from the ordinary man and, according to the traditional boast of heroic epic, grants him a sort of immortality, is, in Vergil's world, hard to distinguish from simple blood lust or battle madness. The Candida Massa, who submit to the saint who urges them to surrender to *amor laudis,* are persuaded by the same fatal rhetoric of glory. Like Nisus and Euryalus, they will attempt to buy their *decus* (glory) at the price of their own blood. The *Spiritus Dei,* working through Cyprian, a man experienced in the ways of seduction, takes the place of the Vergilian gods in instilling *dira cupido* (fatal desire) in the hearts of the Carthaginian people.

Prudentius' treatment of the Candida Massa is rather ironic. They are characterized in the poem as a *grex,* "flock," and Cyprian sees himself as their shepherd, as we see from his prayer from the Tyrian prison:

> da quoque ne quis iners sit de grege quem tuum regebam,
> ne cadat impatiens poenae titubetve quis tuorum,
> incolumen ut numerum reddam tibi debitumque solvam.
>
> *(Perist.* 13.67–69)

Grant too that none of the flock I keep for you is lazy, and that no one of yours falls or stumbles because he cannot bear the punishment. Let me bring the whole group back and dissolve my debt to you.

Cyprian thus assumes a standard, indeed a clichéd, role for a Christian bishop: the good shepherd who carefully guides (*regebam*) his flock (*grege*). There is something sheep-like, as the word *grex* suggests, about the Candida Massa, whose most notable quality is their herd instinct. They move and think *en masse* without the slightest deviation (compare the very different behavior of Hippolytus' followers, who wander all over the landscape searching for pieces of his body). It is, perhaps, a bit of a joke to find that they are so easily persuaded by Cyprian's rhetoric, which offers them a way to transcend their collectivism and attain *decus egregium (Perist.* 13.73), the (unsheep-like) glory of the hero whose deeds separate him from the common herd. Cyprian promises them distinction in death, but the *discrimen sanguinis* (distinction at the price of their blood) he mentions proves to be just as deceptive in the end as the *dura discrimina* that "solved" the riddle of the indistinguishable twins, Larides and Thymber (above, Chapter 2).

The fate of the Candida Massa is not to achieve heroic distinction through martyrdom, but rather to merge together into an indistinguishable mass of raw matter, as we can see in the description Prudentius gives us of their death:

> fama refert foveam campi in medio patere iussam,
> calce vaporifera summos prope margines refertam;
> saxa recocta vomunt ignem niveusque pulvis ardet,
> urere tacta potens et mortifer ex odore flatus.
> adpositam memorant aram fovea stetisse summa
> lege sub hac, salis aut micam, iecur aut suis litarent
> Christicolae, aut mediae sponte inruerent in ima fossae.
> prosiluere alacres cursu rapido simul trecenti,
> gurgite pulvereo mersos liquor aridus voravit
> praecipitemque globum fundo tenus implicavit imo.
> corpora candor habet, candor vehit ad superna mentes,
> "Candida Massa" dehinc dici meruit per omne saeclum.
>
> (*Perist.* 13.76–87)

It is said that a ditch was ordered to be opened up in the middle of a field, filled almost to its upper edges with steaming lime. Baking rocks vomit fire and the white dust flames, able to burn at a touch and deadly to breathe. They recall that an altar was erected at the edge of the pit, with this condition: that the Christians offer a grain of salt or a pig's liver, or else plunge themselves voluntarily into the bottom of the pit. Instantly, eagerly, all three hundred raced together and threw themselves in. A dry liquid swallowed them up when they sank into the dusty vortex, and folded them together into a headlong mass at the pit's lower depths. Glowing heat has their bodies, glowing heat carries their minds to the heavens: that is why they deserved to be called the Glowing Mass throughout the ages.

This martyrdom is not without its comic element. Line 83, which recounts the actual leap into the lime pit, begins with an absurdly galloping rhythm that seems to echo the hooves of a herd of animals and ends with a series of spondees that evoke the long fall into the sea of lime: *prosiluere alacres cursu rapido simul trecenti.*

The terms of the martyrdom are strange as well. After the pit is dug and filled with burning lime, an altar is erected, and the Candida Massa are given the choice between sacrificing a grain of salt or a pig's liver, or else leaping *voluntarily* (*sponte*) into the pit. Leap they do, and with alacrity, but Prudentius' odd inclusion of *sponte* in the magistrate's order raises the question whether being ordered to volunteer for death somehow lessens the voluntarism of the decision. Aristotle, in the *Nicomachean Ethics,* discusses exactly this kind of dubious choice:

> But there is some doubt about actions done through fear of a worse alternative, or for some noble object—as for instance if a tyrant having a man's parents and children in his power commands him to do something base, when if he complies their lives would be spared, but if he refuses they will be put to death. It is open to question whether such actions are voluntary or involuntary. . . . Sometimes indeed men are actually praised for deeds of this "mixed" class, namely when they submit to some disgrace or pain as the price of some great or noble object. (*Nic. Eth.* 3.1.5–7)[22]

The Candida Massa's choice is somewhere between voluntary and involuntary. Like the many senators of the early principate who were ordered by the emperor to commit suicide, their only way of asserting their free will is to collaborate in their own death. So they take the magistrate's order quite literally: they dash eagerly (*alacres*) forward together at top speed (*cursu rapido*) into the pit. Before they hit bottom, they have been transformed from an eager crowd of people into a *praecipitem globum,* a "headlong mass."

There are several paradoxical features in Prudentius' de-

[22]Aristotle, *Nicomachean Ethics,* rev. ed., Eng. trans. by H. Rackham (Cambridge, Mass., 1962).

scription of the lime pit. Most noticeable, perhaps, is the confusion of elements in the fiery pit—all four elements are present, but they exchange properties in a peculiar way. Rocks
belch forth fire; dust is both snowy and burning; air, which
ought to represent the animating breath of life, is *mortifer*
(deadly); and the three hundred are finally swallowed up in a
dusty sea of dry liquid (*gurgite pulvereo mersos liquor aridus
voravit*, line 84). The Candida Massa's death is strangely like
the opening scene from Ovid's *Metamorphoses:*

> ante mare et terras et, quod tegit omnia, caelum
> unus erat toto naturae vultus in orbe,
> quem dixere Chaos, rudis indigestaque moles,
> nec quicquam nisi pondus iners congestaque eodem
> non bene iunctarum discordia semina rerum. . . .
> utque erat et tellus illic et pontus et aer,
> sic erat instabilis tellus, innabilis unda,
> lucis egens aer, nulli sua forma manebat,
> obstabatque aliis aliud, quia corpore in uno
> frigida pugnabant calidis, umentia siccis,
> mollia cum duris, sine pondere habentia pondus.
> hanc deus et melior litem natura diremit;
> nam caelo terras et terris abscidit undas
> et liquidum spisso secrevit ab aere caelum;
> quae postquam evolvit caecoque exemit acervo,
> dissociata locis concordi pace ligavit.
>
> (*Met.* 1.5–10, 15–25)

Before the sea, before the land, before the sky which covers all,
nature had but one face in the world, which they called Chaos—
a raw, unseparated mass. There was nothing but dead weight
and the discordant seeds of things badly joined together. . . .
There was earth there, and sea, and air, but the earth could not
be walked upon; the waves were unswimmable; the air lacked
light: nothing kept its own form. Each thing opposed all others,
for in the same body cold things battled with hot ones, wet with
dry, soft with hard, those with no weight with those which had
weight. God—or a better nature—ended this struggle, dividing
the earth from the sky and the waves from the earth, and sepa-

rating the transparent sky from the dense air. When he had released all things and freed them from the blind heap, he bound the discordant elements in their places with peaceful harmony.

The opening of the *Metamorphoses* depicts the world before the creation. Nothing exists except raw matter, the four elements in an indistinguishable mass (*rudis indigestaque moles*), inseparable and entirely without form. Air, water, and earth are all present, but they lack their proper characteristics—the earth cannot be stood upon, the waves are unswimmable, the air lacks light. The fiery pit that swallows up the Candida Massa re-creates this primeval chaos: its rocks produce fire, its dust is like snow, and its liquid is dry. But there is a significant difference between Ovid's chaos and Prudentius' pit. Ovid shows us the world before its creation, and we see its progress as the creator god (or nature) divides the elements and brings the universe into being, starting with the division into heaven, earth, and sea, and ending with the creation of humanity. Prudentius, in this scene, shows us the process in reverse. Instead of the creation of mankind out of raw matter, we see three hundred individuals melted down into a single entity, a lump whose shining whiteness makes it indistinguishable from the dissolving lime that engulfs it. There is no *discrimen* here, nothing but the chaos that is the raw material of the universe, unformed and preexistent.

This is the ultimate expression of the power that characterizes Cyprian in this poem, the merging power that destroys differences and denies separation, the power of eros without any form of restraint. The melting down of the Candida Massa is also the ironic fulfillment of the peculiar subjunctive clause that describes Cyprian in the first line of the poem—*Punica terra tulit, quo splendeat omne, quidquid usquam est* (the Punic earth bore him to make everything everywhere shine). One might expect Cyprian to inspire religious fervor in his followers, but who could anticipate that it would lead to the fiery end of the Candida Massa? The confusion of the elements in the fiery pit, and the destruction of individuality in the Candida Massa itself, helps to explain the vague and awkward abstraction of *omne, quidquid usquam est*—once again, Prudentius uses peculiar syntax to call attention to (in this case, to adumbrate) an issue of thematic importance in his verse, and once again, as in the passage of the *Hamartigenia* in which he conceals his boastful anagram, we get a glimpse of his sardonic humor.

Ashes and Dust

Lime, a mixture of fire and earth, is a most appropriate substance to represent Chaos in this poem, which shows us life moving backward into inert matter. Indeed, the lime that dissolves flesh, the crucible in which the Candida Massa are reduced to a glowing mass, is a curious substance, and one that plays an important role in Greek accounts of the death of Dionysus. Marcel Detienne, in his *Dionysus Slain*, shows the connection between lime and the Titans, the earthborn enemies of the gods, in this summary of the evidence (he is discussing the reason the Titans are said to be covered with gypsum, a white dust, when they slay the infant Dionysus):

Technically speaking, gypsum (*gupsos*) is a plaster the Greeks rarely used as paint. . . . But this stone is often associated, not to say confused, with quicklime, a substance obtained by heating marble and limestone in kilns. It happens that the specific word for "quicklime" in Greek is *titanos*, or "titan," which signifies the whitish dust, the kind of white ash produced by the firing of any kind of limestone. Consequently, the murderers masked in gypsum—are they not in fact hidden by that which best reveals their identity? The supposition is apparently supported by certain traditions concerning the existence of the first autochthonous people, sometimes called *Titan*, sometimes *Titenios* or *Titakos*. . . .

All these traditions concern beings born from the earth and, in particular, formed from the earthly element mixed with the fire designated by their name *titanos*, quicklime. The Titan of

Sikyon has the sun as his brother. . . . This mixture of fire and earth is also a physical fact recorded in Aristotle's *Meteorologica:* "Bodies formed from earth are mostly hot as a consequence of the heat that produced them, for example quicklime and ash, *titanos kai tephra.*" But Eustathios' commentaries on Homeric epic preserve a much more precise relationship between the first autochthonous creatures called Titans and the enemies of Dionysos covered with whitish dust. In the margins of the Iliadic lines that invoke the white peaks of Titanos, the learned archbishop of Thessalonika reminds us that *titanos* is the technical term for quicklime, and that this name comes directly from the punishment suffered in the myth of the Titans when they were reduced to ashes by Zeus's fire and mingled with the white dust produced by the firing of lime and marble.[23]

In this myth about the Titans, the mixture of fire and earth marks both their origin and their eventual destruction—they are created from fire mixed with earth, and in the end Zeus' thunderbolt reduces them to ashes and quicklime. Like the Candida Massa, they are reduced from living beings to the raw material from which they came.

Cyprian himself shows some Titanic characteristics in the poem. He is born from the Punic earth (*Punica terra tulit*), and he is consistently associated with fire—he makes young brides seethe with passion (*aestuante*, line 24); he sets the hearts of his followers aflame (line 49); and he makes them burn with the desire for martyrdom (line 72). His judge berates him at the end of the poem (after the Candida Massa, like the Titans, have been reduced to earth and fire) for denying Zeus' thunderbolt, the same weapon that destroys the Titans in the Dionysian myth. Indeed, it is precisely this consistent emphasis on fire and earth that seems to have been Prudentius' reason for linking Cyprian with the Candida Massa in the first place—a connection, as I have noted, that only Prudentius makes—and for his invention of the Candida Massa's strange martyrdom and dissolution into white dust. And, as so often in Prudentius'

[23]Detienne, *Dionysos Slain,* trans. Mireille Muellner and Leonard Muellner (Baltimore, 1979), pp. 80–81.

poems, the key to solving the puzzle is an etymological word-play. Cyprian's character in the poem is determined by his Latin name, Cyprianus; we have seen how Prudentius has presented him as an erotic figure. But Cyprian has another name as well: Thascius, an apparently Punic name whose meaning is not known. It is at least likely that Prudentius associated the name Thascius with the Latin word *tasconium*, which Pliny tells us means a kind of white earth,[24] for he introduces it into the poem immediately after he has explained how the Candida Massa received their name from their dissolution in the limepit:

> "Candida Massa" dehinc dici meruit per omne saeclum.
> laetior interea iam Thascius ob diem suorum . . .
>
> $$(13.87-88)$$

> That is why they deserved to be called the Glowing Mass throughout the ages. Thascius, meanwhile, happier because of the fate of his people . . .

Thus the two parts of Cyprian's name explain the peculiar plot of the poem. His first name, which links him to Venus, makes him the erotic hero of the first part of the poem; his Punic name associates him with lime, the white earth that has the power to dissolve bodies, and so with the Candida Massa.

Prudentius has, in the figure of Cyprian, combined a number of traditions with some inventions of his own and has woven together a fabric of traditional motifs that combine to create the unexpected. This poem, more than any of the others in the *Peristephanon*, is a reflection on martyrdom itself. And, despite the incongruity of finding a critique of martyrdom within a hymn to a martyr, we are forced, it seems to me, to conclude from this poem that Prudentius was strongly—even bitterly—opposed to certain kinds of martyrdom, such as that motivated by the urge for self-destruction or by mis-

---

[24]According to the *Oxford Latin Dictionary* entry, *tasconium* is probably borrowed into Latin from Iberian, which makes it more likely that Prudentius, a Spaniard, would be familiar with it.

guided passion. He uses every possible means to associate martyrdom with suicide and with sterile eroticism in this poem, taking full advantage of Carthage's portrayal in literature as a city of suicide and mad love. He presents us with a Cyprian who is a beautiful youth associated with magic spells and love charms, whose erotic power is sterile and destructive. Prudentius suggests his sterility by alluding to the cutting of the *caesaries,* a theme developed by Statius as an emblem of castration and death; by opposing him to normal marriage when he shows him attacking the productive marriage bed; and by showing his abrupt transformation from beautiful, sexually excessive youth to old age. The Candida Massa, Cyprian's sheep-like followers, hurl themselves into a pit of lime, and instead of earning the *decus egregium* (outstanding glory) they anticipate, they are annihilated in a scene that reverses the description of the creation of humanity from chaos in Ovid's *Metamorphoses,* thus demonstrating again that Cyprian's powers of erotic persuasion result in destruction rather than in life.

Prudentius, through his manipulation of traditional motifs and allusions to earlier authors, has created a poem that reveals the perverse eroticism and the suicidal compulsion that characterize a certain kind of martyrdom. Though he does not mention the Donatists by name (Prudentius rarely mentions current heresies in his poems), the African setting of the poem and the choice of Cyprian, the Donatists' favorite martyr, as the subject suggest that the growing schism in the African church and the Donatists' well-known predilection for martyrdom may well have been the inspiration for the poem. The Candida Massa, indeed, are almost a caricature of the Circumcellions, the extremists who roamed in mobs from martyr's shrine to martyr's shrine (each shrine, be it noted, marked by whitewash),[25] invoking the name of Cyprian and committing suicide in the name of martyrdom.[26]

[25]W. H. C. Frend, "The *Cellae* of the African Circumcellions," pp. 87–89.

[26]Augustine, indeed, refers to groups of Circumcellions committing suicide in mass leaps from mountaintops and cliffs and uses language very similar to Prudentius' description of the Candida Massa (*Contra Gaudentium* 1.28.32).

6

Saint Agnes and the Chaste Tree

Peristephanon 13, the martyrdom of Cyprian, has as its mythical-historic background the foundation myth of Carthage: the suicide of Dido and the Phoenician custom of infant sacrifice. *Peristephanon* 14, in many ways a counterpoint to the Cyprian poem, has as its subtext the foundation myth of Rome: the birth of the twins Romulus and Remus to the Vestal Virgin, their exposure after birth, and their adoption by the friendly she-wolf who nurtured them. In this chapter we will explore the associations between Agnes, the virgin martyr, and certain aspects of the Romulus myth, but first we will examine the emphasis throughout the poem on the motif of binding and loosing—a motif that plays an essential role in Prudentius' poetry, as we have seen in the previous chapters.

In *Peristephanon* 11 Hippolytus is first bound by his executioners, then caught in the knots of the horses' reins, and finally, in a dramatic reversal of the bondage imagery, torn asunder and scattered in fragments over a landscape drenched in his blood.[1] Cyprian is characterized throughout *Peristephanon* 13 by language of release and dissolution, but his flowing eloquence has the paradoxical effect of binding his followers so tightly together that they end up fused into a single glowing mass in an episode that parodies the creation scene of Ovid's *Metamorphoses* 1.[2] In *Peristephanon* 14, language of binding and

[1] *Perist.* 11.95ff.
[2] *Perist.* 13.70–84.

149

release again plays a dominant role and is closely connected to Agnes' role in the poem as a virginal prostitute.[3]

The opening lines of *Peristephanon* 14, which describe Agnes' tomb and her role as a protector of Rome, set the tone for the constrictive, confining language of the rest of the poem:

> Agnes sepulcrum est Romulea in domo,
> fortis puellae, martyris inclytae.
> conspectu in ipso condita turrium
> servat salutem virgo Quiritium,
> nec non et ipsos protegit advenas
> puro ac fideli pectore supplices.
> duplex corona est praestita martyri:
> intactum ab omni crimine virginal,
> mortis deinde gloria liberae.
>
> *(Perist.* 14.1–9)

Inside the house of Romulus lies the tomb of Agnes, a forceful girl and a famous martyr. Buried deep in the foundations, in sight of the towers, the virgin watches over the health of the

[3]The best overview of the various Agnes legends is in Alexander Denomy's *Old French Lives of Saint Agnes* (Cambridge, Mass., 1938); in his introduction he lists the earliest sources and weighs their historicity. The earliest sources for the story of Agnes are Ambrose's *De Virginibus* 1.2 (written ca. 377; *PL* 16 cols. 200–202), in which he praises the saint for her virginity and her bravery (*et virgo permansit et martyrium obtinuit:* she both remained a virgin and achieved martyrdom); and a hymn attributed to Ambrose, written sometime in the last quarter of the fourth century (*PL* 17 col. 1210), *Agnes Beatae Virginis* (which, as Denomy points out, is considerably influenced by Ovid's account of the death of Polyxena in *Met.* 13.439–493). Finally, there is an epigram by Pope Damasus (*PL* 13 cols. 402–403), written between 366 and 384 and probably seen by Prudentius. In none of these sources is there any mention of the most striking features of Prudentius' account of Agnes' martyrdom: her condemnation to a public brothel and her attack on the anonymous young man who is struck down by a thunderbolt. These details, as I shall argue, were taken from stories attached to other virgins and linked to Agnes by Prudentius, who once again seems to select a plot based on an elaborate series of wordplays on his saint's name. As it happened, the brothel element became one of the major features of the Agnes legend as it was developed in the Middle Ages. (One later development not in Prudentius is the story that Agnes, when forced to stand naked in public, was granted a miracle—her hair grew spontaneously to cover her.)

people of Quirinus. She protects strangers too, who come as suppliants with pure and faithful hearts. A double-twisted crown is offered to the martyr: one strand for her virginity, untouched by any crime, and the other for her death's liberating glory.

Agnes, though described as the patron and protector of Rome, is defined and confined by the poet's language of restraint, as if her presence is felt as a dangerous force that needs to be contained. In the first line, *Agnes sepulcrum est Romulea in domo*, Agnes is doubly confined, in her tomb and in the house, *domo*, of Romulus. In line 3 the perspective shifts, and we find the tomb itself is surrounded by the towers of the city: *conspectu in ipso condita turrium. Condita*, meaning "buried" or "hidden," is particularly appropriate here after the mention of Romulus because it is also the word used for the foundation of the city, as in the common phrase *ab urbe condita*. The conjunction of this verb, the mention of Romulus, and the tomb's location in the center of Rome suggests that the tomb of Agnes is somehow intimately connected with the origins of the city.

In line 4 the emphasis shifts somewhat from the language of enclosure and confinement to that of protection and shelter, as Agnes moves from being the passive recipient to being the active agent. She preserves (*servat*, line 4) and protects (or covers over, *protegit*, line 5) both Romans and strangers (*advenas*, line 5).

Agnes is thus safely enclosed at the beginning of the poem, triply buried in the heart of the city of Romulus. She is granted her *duplex corona*, "double-twisted crown," for two things, her untouched virginity and her voluntary (or liberating) death. Virginity and death are inextricably entwined in the image of the double crown, and they are linked by this image to Prudentius' own literary efforts as well, for the *corona* Agnes receives is his poem about her—the last of the strands that make up the poetic garland of the *Peristephanon*.

After the introduction, Prudentius describes the trials of the young saint. She is a girl of scarcely marriageable age who refuses to sacrifice to idols—in this case, she is offered a choice between laying down her head at the altar of Minerva and being exposed in a public brothel. (This strange punishment is, as we shall see, one of a series of plays on Agnes' name, which Prudentius associates with the Greek *hagne*, "chaste," as well as with the Latin *agna*, "lamb".) Sure of her invincible chastity, Agnes refuses to make the token gesture to Minerva and is sentenced to be exposed in a *lupanar*, "brothel." The crowd that gathers, touched by her piety, is ashamed to look at her nakedness, except for one nameless young man who rashly looks on her with lascivious intent (*lumine lubrico*, line 54). He is immediately struck by a bolt of lightning and left for dead in the square until Agnes takes pity on him and restores his senses. This incident infuriates the judge, who orders Agnes put to the sword. Agnes receives this news with delight, delivers a speech in which she rapturously welcomes her executioner as a lover, and fantasizes about receiving his sword deep in her breast. Instead of the erotic death she envisions, by sword thrust, Agnes is beheaded, and her spirit, liberated from the body, leaps up to heaven accompanied by a crowd of angels.

In the brothel scene we can see once again the tension between imagery of confinement and imagery of release. The judge, described as a *trux tyrannus*, says he will have Agnes thrust into a public brothel, *hanc in lupanar trudere publicum* (line 25), if she does not perform the required ritual sacrifice. Once again, the idea is to confine Agnes, to keep her enclosed, but he does not follow through with his planned confinement. She is put not inside, but rather in a corner of a public square, *in flexu plateae*, and is thus exposed rather than enclosed. It is at this point, when the confining language of the poem is temporarily absent, that Agnes is able to reverse the polarities of the poem. Until now the subject of linguistic and judicial restraint, she is suddenly able to command a power that moves outward. Her sudden access of power is linked to two elements, fire and water—the winged flame of the thunderbolt, which strikes the young man, and the prayers that flow, *fudisse*, to heal him.

But this sudden explosion of Agnes' power is immediately curtailed by the language of the poem. After the youth is restored to health, the entire brothel scene is spatially re-defined by the metaphor in lines 61–63:

> primum sed Agnes hunc habuit gradum
> caelestis aulae, mox alius datur
> ascensus.
> > *(Perist.* 14.61–63)

This was Agnes' first step towards the heavenly palace, but soon she was granted another step upwards.

Agnes' exposure and burst of apparently liberating power is recast as the first step on the way to the palace of heaven, *caelestis aulae.* Once again the language of the poem attempts to confine her, to place her inside an enclosed space—first the house of Romulus, then a brothel, and finally the heavenly palace.

The opposition between inward and outward movement reaches its climax in Agnes' final speech (as does the sexual imagery that pervades the poem). It is clear from her language that Agnes, like her judge, considers herself a woman en-closed. The judge, when condemning her to the brothel, imag-ined the youth of the town rushing *in* to claim her (*omnis iuventus inruet*), and Agnes echoes the verb *inruo* when she imagines herself meeting the executioner, who plays the role of rapist/lover in her imagination:

> hic, hic amator iam, fateor, placet:
> ibo inruentis gressibus obviam.
> > *(Perist.* 14.74–75)

Now I confess it—this man is the lover who pleases me! When he forces himself on me, I will meet him halfway.

She pictures her death, in the same speech, as a form of inward movement, as a rape or penetration, imagining the executioner's sword penetrating her breast as she draws all its strength (or violence, *vim*) deep within her:

> nec demorabor vota calentia:
> ferrum in papillas omne recepero
> pectusque ad imum vim gladii traham.
> $\qquad\qquad$ (*Perist.* 14.76–78)

I will not put off (his?) burning desire: I will take his whole sword into my breasts and draw the force of his blade deep into my heart.

Chaste Agnes' sudden shift to violently erotic language, which parallels her exposure as a prostitute, has a classical precedent in the *Phaedra*. Theseus, horrified by the story of Hippolytus' supposed rape of Phaedra, recalls the violent alternation between absolute chastity and promiscuity that characterized the Amazons, one of whom was Hippolytus' mother.[4]

Erotic implications aside, Agnes believes the executioner's penetrating sword will enable her to leap away, to transcend her earthly confinements. Her dizzying leap into the heavens seems to put her beyond the possibility of confinement, but once again the language of the poem is ambiguous even in her final prayer for release:

[4]Seneca *Phaedra* 908–914, 920–922:

> est prorsus iste gentis armiferae furor
> odisse Venus foedera et castum diu
> vulgare populis corpus. o tetrum genus
> nullaque victum lege melioris soli!
> ferae quoque ipsae Veneris evitant nefas
> generisque leges inscius servat pudor. . . .
> pudor impudentem celat, audacem quies,
> pietas nefandum; vera fallaces probant,
> simulantque molles dura.

It is surely the madness of that weapon-bearing tribe [the Amazons] to hate the alliances of Venus and to share a body, too long chaste, with the mob. O foul race, bound by the law of no better land! Even the beasts themselves avoid unspeakable love, and their ignorant modesty preserves the laws of their kind. . . . Shame conceals the shameless; silence, audacity; piety, the unspeakable. Liars applaud the truth, and the soft masquerade as hard.

aeterne rector, divide ianuas
caeli obseratas terrigenis prius,
ac te sequentem, Christe, animam voca,
cum virginalem, tum Patris hostiam.

(*Perist.* 14.81–84)

Eternal ruler, open up the gates of heaven, closed until now to
dwellers on earth, and call the soul, O Christ, that follows you—
a virgin, and the Father's sacrificial victim.

Though Agnes appears to be asking for freedom—un-
locked gates, opened doors—she is, topologically, envisioning
the opposite, for she imagines herself *outside* the doors trying
to get *inside*. These lines pick up the image noted above in lines
61–62, in which her miracle is redefined as the first step on the
way into the *caelestis aulae*. Once again the outward movement—in the first case, her command of the thunderbolt, in
this case, her soul's transcendent leap—is shown, from another perspective, to be a movement in.

The stroke of the executioner's sword releases Agnes' spirit
which, as it flies upward, takes on the flashing movement of
flame:

exutus inde spiritus emicat
liberque in auras exilit. angeli
saepsere euntem tramite candido.

(*Perist.* 14.91–93)

Her spirit flashes forth and leaps free into the air. Angels fence
her in as she goes along the shining path.

The sense of outward movement dominates lines 91 and 92,
reinforced by the triple use of verbs with the prefix *ex-* or *e-*:
exutus, emicat, exilit. The sound pattern, however, undermines
the liberating sense, for Agnes' free spirit is enclosed between
the *ex-* compounds at the beginning and the end of the sentence. The confining sound pattern, with its harsh *x, c,* and *t*
sounds, prepares us for the next line, in which Agnes' flashing,
outward movement is met by a powerful containing force, the

angels who surround her (*saepsere*) as she goes. Agnes is thus continually confined and enclosed, forced, despite her occasional outbreaks, to inhabit interior space. The oscillation between interior and exterior space, and outward and inward movement, is a topological expression of Agnes' ambivalent position in the poem.

A Wolf in Sheep's Clothing?

We have already seen that the first line of the poem links Agnes with Romulus, the founder of Rome. In the brothel scene, there is another link with the Romulus legend. Though there are many variations, the standard version of Rome's foundation myth makes Romulus and Remus the sons of the god Mars and a Vestal Virgin named either Rhea Silvia or Ilia. The twins are exposed at birth and adopted by a she-wolf who nurses them and raises them until they are found by a shepherd. The strange doubling of the mother figure, who is split into virgin and *lupa* (she-wolf), is one of the most striking features of the story, and it did not escape the Romans that *lupa* means prostitute as well as she-wolf. Livy points it out in his version of the story:

Vi compressa Vestalis, cum geminum partum edidisset, seu ita rata seu quia deus auctor culpae honestior erat, Martem incertae stirpis patrem nuncupat. Sed nec dii nec homines aut ipsam aut stirpem a crudelitate regia vindicant: sacerdos vincta in custodiam datur: pueros in profluentem aquam mitti iubet. . . . Tenet fama, cum fluitantem alveum quo expositi erant pueri tenuis in sicco aqua destituisset, lupam sitientem ex montibus qui circa sunt ad puerilem vagitum cursum flexisse; eam summissas infantibus adeo mitem praebuisse mammas ut lingua lambentem pueros magister regii pecoris invenerit, Faustulo fuisse nomen ferunt. Ab ea stabula Larentiae uxori educandos datos. Sunt qui Larentiam vulgato corpore lupam inter pastores vocatam putent; inde locum fabulae ac miraculo datum. (Livy 1.4.2–8)

The Vestal was raped, and when she had given birth to twins, she named Mars as the parent of her questionable offspring, whether because she really thought so, or because it seemed more noble for a god to commit such a crime. But neither the gods nor men were able to save the mother and the children from the king's cruelty: the priestess was bound and thrown in prison, and the children were ordered to be committed to the flowing river. . . . The story goes that when the basket in which the children had been exposed was grounded in the shallow water, a thirsty wolf coming from the mountains turned her steps towards the infants' wailing. She offered them her breasts so gently that the keeper of the king's flocks (his name, they say, was Faustulus) found her licking them with her tongue. He took them from there to his hut and gave them to his wife Larentia to raise. There are those who think that Larentia, who had slept around freely, was called a prostitute (*lupa*) by the shepherds, and that this was the start of the miraculous story.

The same doubling occurs in Prudentius' poem, for Agnes, the untouched virgin, is forced to assume the role of a prostitute, making her, etymologically, both a virginal whore and a sheep (*agnus*) in wolf's clothing. Neither Ambrose nor Damasus, both of whom wrote hymns to Saint Agnes, mentions her trial by brothel, though her virginity is important in both poems. As I discuss in more detail later, there is in Palladius' *Lausiac History* a similar story about a virgin sentenced to a brothel who, through God's intervention, manages to escape with her chastity intact, but Prudentius appears to be the first to associate this story with Agnes.[5]

Agnes' sexual nature is central to the poem, just as Cyprian's sterile eroticism was to *Peristephanon* 13. The first piece of information we learn about her concerns her readiness for marriage:

[5]Palladius *Hist. Laus.* 65. A similar story appears also in Nicephoros Callistus (*Ecclesiastica Historia*) 7.13, in which the young man is decapitated. The story is associated with Agnes in the Latin Passion of St. Agnes (*AASS* vol. 2 January 714–718), which is agreed to be later than Prudentius' poem. (See John Francis Petrucione, "Prudentius' Use of Martyrological Topoi in *Peristephanon*," diss., University of Michigan, 1985, pp. 101–102.)

aiunt iugali vix habilem toro
primis in annis forte puellulam
Christo calentem fortiter inpiis
iussis renisam, quo minus idolis
addicta sacram desereret fidem.

(Perist. 14.10–14)

They say she was scarcely ready to bear the yoke of marriage—a
little girl in her first youth who happened to burn for Christ, and
boldly refused the impious order to vow herself to idols and
desert the holy faith.

   Prudentius' Agnes is an adolescent, scarcely out of her child-
hood (*primis in annis*). It is a familiar topos in Roman poetry, as
we saw in Chapter 5, that adolescence is a time of wavering,
uncertain identity, when sexuality is polymorphous and un-
determined, when girls and boys seem indistinguishable. It is a
dangerous state, linked again and again in the poetic corpus to
death or sterility, as the sad fates of Euryalus, Camilla, Narcissus, and the unfortunate Earinus (castrated to preserve his
beauty) attest. Agnes, described as a *puellulam,* a younger and
more innocent version of the *puella* of standard erotic poetry,
belongs to this list of doomed youths. She is ready for marriage, but only barely (*vix habilem toro*); her age and sexual state
define her in the poem. It is not until we have learned these
things about her that we find she is *Christo calentem.* "burning
for Christ," and it is clear that her passion is an erotic one—the
use of flames and heat as metaphors for sexual desire is too
familiar to need documentation.
   As the poem progresses, Agnes' trial and sentencing take on
some of the aspects of a courtship:

temptata multis nam prius artibus.
nunc ore blandi iudicis inlice,
nunc saevientis carnificis minis,
stabat feroci robore pertinax
corpusque duris excruciatibus
ultro offerebat, non renuens mori.

(Perist. 14.15–20)

Already subjected to many artful temptations—first the seductive speech of the suave judge, then threats of a savage executioner—she stood stubborn in her fierce strength, and freely
gave her body to the rack, nodding yes to death.

Agnes is faced with a judge who speaks like a lover and with
an executioner whom she later welcomes as a lover. The judge
and the executioner, though separate characters in the poem,
are similar; the same adjective, *trux,* is used to describe both of
them.[6] The interchangeability of the judge, who operates
through seductive rhetoric, and the executioner, who relies on
physical force, emphasizes the pervasive confusion in this
poem between seduction and death, exposing rhetoric and
violence as two aspects of a single, violent process of coercion.

With a sublimating logic that would have delighted Freud,
the trial scene unfolds. Agnes, refusing to succumb to the
blandishments of the judge, offers herself willingly to the
carnifex (executioner) and his tortures, with the same sponta-
neous passion that led the Candida Massa to leap voluntarily
to their collective death in *Peristephanon* 13. The judge then
replaces his threats of death with the punishment of public
prostitution. Finally, when Agnes emerges unscathed from
the brothel, she reverses the judge's substitution of rape for
death by imagining her death as the ultimate form of sexual
experience.

Agnes is sentenced to exposure in the brothel for a very specific crime, her refusal to touch her head to the altar of Minerva and ask forgiveness for neglecting to worship her. The
sudden appearance of Minerva in the poem reveals the extent
to which Prudentius relied, consciously or unconsciously, on
mythological paradigms in his poetry. Here is the relevant
passage:

> tum trux tyrannus: "si facile est," ait,
> "poenam subactis ferre doloribus

[6]For a discussion of tyrants and judges in Prudentius, see Ilona Opelt, "Der
Christenverfolger bei Prudentius," *Philologus* 111 (1967):242–257.

et vita vilis spernitur, at pudor
carus dicatae virginitatis est.
hanc in lupanar trudere publicum
certum est, ad aram ni caput applicat
ac de Minerva iam veniam rogat,
quam virgo pergit temnere virginem."
                    (*Perist.* 14.21–28)

Then the fierce tyrant says, "If she finds it easy to endure the
pain of such punishment, and despises her own life as something worthless, at least her chastity, as a vowed virgin, is valu-
able to her. I will surely have her thrust into a public brothel if
she does not touch her head to the altar and ask pardon of
Minerva, the virgin goddess whom she, a virgin, scorns."

Prudentius casts Agnes' refusal to submit to authority as an
offense against Minerva specifically. His judge finds it odd that
Agnes, as a virgin, would scorn Minerva, a virgin goddess, and
this remark points to one of the issues that underlies the poem,
Agnes' sexual ambivalence. For Agnes' virginity is radically
different from Minerva's, or, to use her Greek name, Athena's.
Athena's virginity, and the peculiar story of her birth from the
head of Zeus, set her apart from other female figures and mark
her as an exemplar of co-opted femininity. Zeus gave birth to
his prodigious child after he had swallowed her mother, Metis,
when he learned from an oracle that Metis' son would be
greater than his father.[7] By swallowing Metis, whose name
means "intelligence," Zeus incorporated her binding power
and cunning intelligence into himself. Instead of Metis pro-
ducing the strong son he feared, Zeus himself gives birth to the
martial goddess Athena, whose birth from the head of Zeus
shows her to be an unmediated extension of her father's nature. Zeus' incorporation of the mother somehow resulted in
the transformation of the child from feared male rival to obe-
dient daughter—a daughter, moreover, whose vow of per-

[7]See Marcel Detienne and Jean-Paul Vernant, *Cunning Intelligence in Greek
Culture and Society,* trans. Janet Lloyd (Brighton, 1978), pp. 14ff., for a
discussion of Zeus and Metis.

petual virginity effectively prevents her from coming under the control of any other male. Athena is a goddess who receives the trappings of male power, but only after she has rejected her own sexuality—she is, essentially, neutered.[8]

It is, perhaps, Minerva's head-birth that accounts for her peculiar affinity for disembodied heads. If we think for a moment about some of the myths that cluster around the goddess, we may conclude that Agnes' refusal to submit her head to the goddess' power was a wise precaution. The story of Arachne in Ovid's *Metamorphoses* is a case in point.[9] Arachne, a virgin who excels in the craft of weaving (inevitably associated in ancient poetry with the act of poetic creation) attracts the anger of the jealous goddess, who challenges her to a weaving contest. Arachne weaves a tapestry that is a bitter and detailed indictment of various misdeeds, deceits, and rapes committed by the male gods. The tapestry Pallas weaves is a pointed reminder of the absolute power the gods have over humans. The contest ends in a draw (though Ovid undoubtedly favors Arachne), and Pallas, furious at Arachne's undeniable talent, transforms her into a spider and condemns her to a life suspended by a thread. She is doomed to weave the threads of her own prison for eternity, trapped forever in the confines of her loom.

Like Agnes, Arachne is a virgin opposed to Minerva, and her punishment is formally equivalent to Agnes'. Agnes loses her head; Arachne, transformed into a spider, becomes what looks very much like a disembodied head surrounded by long, tendril-like legs, a shrunken twin of a more famous head constantly associated with the virgin goddess: the petrifying head of the Gorgon Medusa, which appears on the *aegis* Minerva and her father share.

Medusa, as Ovid tells the story, was a virgin who had the

---

[8]The misogynistic elements of the myth are emphasized by Apollo in Aeschylus' *Eumenides*, in which he uses the story of Athena's birth from the head of Zeus to argue that women are unimportant in childbearing (*Eum.* 657–666).

[9]*Met.* 6.1–145.

misfortune to be raped by Poseidon in Minerva's temple. Acting with an irrationality typical of the Ovidian gods, Minerva reacts by punishing the victim: she transforms Medusa's beautiful hair into a nest of snakes, thus apparently endowing her with the fearful power to transform those who look on her to stone. Minerva has another part to play in Medusa's story as well, for it is she who gives Perseus the vital information that enables him to cut off the Gorgon's head without being turned into a statue. After the decapitation, Minerva makes the head the device of her shield, appropriating its terrible apotropaic power. Froma Zeitlin remarks:

> Even without Freud's observations on the head of Medusa, the various spheres of reference to which the Gorgon belongs suggest her identity as a "genitalized" head. Her apotropaic function in war magic is beyond question. . . . In this context the gesture of women in besieged cities who repel the enemy by an act of *anasyrma* (Plutarch, *De Virt. Mul.* 5.9) is analogous in its intention to the role of the Gorgon. This apotropaic effect of the women's act is operative only with regard to the opposite sex (the outsider) and the enemy (potential or actual). The Gorgon can be understood as a means of exploiting female demonic energy in the exposure of its secrets to those who must encounter its frontal gaze and its face of death. This energy immobilizes, paralyzes the male, as the special talent of that most famous Gorgon, Medusa, confirms.[10]

Anasyrma, to which Zeitlin refers, consists of lifting up the skirts to expose the genitals, an act with the same paralyzing effect on the enemy as the face of Medusa has on those who see it.

There are several parallels between the plight of Agnes in this poem and Ovid's Medusa. Both are virgins; both are sexually threatened at the altar of Minerva. Agnes is sent to a brothel, while Medusa is raped. As a result of the violation and exposure, both are endowed with a paralyzing power. Here is

[10]Zeitlin, "Cultic Models of the Female: Rites of Dionysos and Demeter," *Arethusa* 15 (1982):147.

the scene in which Agnes (or perhaps God, in response to her prayers; the agent is unclear) fells the unfortunate voyeur with a thunderbolt:

> sic elocutam publicitus iubet
> flexu in plateae sistere virginem.
> stantem refugit maesta frequentia
> aversa vultus, ne petulantius
> quisquam verendum conspiceret locum.
> intendit unus forte procaciter
> os in puellam nec trepidat sacram
> spectare formam lumine lubrico.
> en ales ignis fulminis in modum
> vibratur ardens atque oculos ferit.
> caecus corusco lumine corruit
> atque in plateae pulvere palpitat.
> (Perist. 14.38–49)

At the end of her speech, he orders the virgin to be exposed in the corner of a public square. The sad crowd flee, turning their faces from her as she stands lest any lewd person should see the fearful place. But one man happens to be bolder: he turns his gaze on the girl, not afraid to leer at her holy body. And look! A winged flame like a thunderbolt, throbbing and burning, strikes his eyes. Blinded by the glittering light, he collapses and twitches in the dust of the square.

Agnes' public nakedness has the same effect as *anasyrma*, paralyzing those who look on it. Even the mention of her exposed genitals is avoided by the neutral periphrasis *verendum locum*.[11] The exposure of what cannot be seen, or even named in the text, charges her with the same demonic female energy as the Gorgon's head.

Not surprisingly, this sudden access of female power is described in the poem in strictly male terms. Agnes is given the attributes of male power and behaves, until she is suppressed,

[11]The virgin in Palladius' parallel account uses a similar periphrasis—she tells her suitors that she has a sore in a *kekrummenon topon*, "hidden place" (*Palladius Hist. Lau.* 65.3).

like Zeus. The brothel scene, in which the young man is para-
lyzed by her nakedness, is a replay of the story of Zeus and
Semele, with the young man cast in the role of Semele. The
thunderbolt that strikes the young man is, of course, Zeus'
favorite weapon, and the phrase Prudentius uses, *en ales ignis
fulminis in modum* (line 46), is an echo of one of Horace's odes,
which begins with a description of another of Zeus' rapes:

> Qualem ministrum fulminis alitem
> cui rex deorum regnum in avis vagas
>   permisit expertus fidelem
>   Iuppiter in Ganymede flavo . . .
>   (*Carm.* 4.4.1–4)

Like the winged bearer of the thunderbolt, to whom Jupiter
gave rule over the wandering birds because of his faithful service
in the affair of blond Ganymede . . .

In the brothel scene, when Agnes escapes momentarily from
the confining language of the poem, she appears in an aggressive, and therefore masculine, role.[12] Her potential attacker is
reduced to the status of rape victim by the allusion to Ganymede, and the phallic power of Agnes' thunderbolt leaves him
blinded and impotent. This sudden acquisition of virile power
raises Agnes from victim to victor. Like a military hero, she
departs from the scene of her battle *triumphans*, celebrating a
military triumph. Her *virginitas* is described as *victrix* (victorious), and her judge drives home the point and completes
the series of wordplays by exclaiming *"vincor!"* (I am conquered!, line 64).

---

[12]There is a similar moment in Seneca the Elder's *Controversiae* 1.2.21,
when a virgin who has been kidnapped and placed in a brothel overcomes a
rapist. Her victory is described in language suggesting both divine intervention and a sex change: "negabat se puella fecisse; negabat illum suis cecidisse
manibus. Altior, inquit, humana visa est circa me species eminere et puellares
lacertos supra virile robur attollere" (The girl denied that she had done it; she
said he had not fallen by her hand. "A shape taller than human seemed to
loom over me, and to raise my girlish arms to a more than masculine
strength," she said).

Saint Agnes and the Chaste Tree

Agnes, if we may think for a moment in Greek terms, represents a threatening deviation from normal sexuality. Virginity, as such, was not highly valued in Greek and Roman society. Marriage was the proper *telos* of the young girl. Once grown to maturity (*teleia*), she was expected to produce children, just as a tree naturally produces fruit.[13] As Detienne has shown, a remarkable number of Greek myths center around the institution of marriage, some dealing with young men and women who attempt to flee from the yoke of marriage—Hippolytus, Melanion, Callisto, and Atalanta, to name a few. These young people, who flee to the wild places and the woods to escape from the civic institution of marriage, occupy what Detienne calls "the terrain of the hunter":

> Forest and mountains compose a masculine landscape from which the woman/wife is radically absent; so, too, are excluded the socio-political values that define the proper use of the female body. In the space where social rules are silent, deviance is articulate, and transgressions come to pass. . . . As a result of its position between war and marriage, the hunter's terrain gains its capacity for becoming the privileged place in myth for marginal sexual behavior, whether it be masculine or feminine denial of marriage, or, inversely, experimentation with censured sexual behavior. As a liminal place where socially dominant sexual relations are as if suspended, the land of the hunt is open to the subversion of amorous pursuits, whatever their process or modality.[14]

Artemis is the goddess who presides over the "terrain of the hunter," and Artemis and her followers offer a model of virginity very much in opposition to the one provided by Athena, who epitomizes civic values and whose essentially sexless nature indicates her complete assimilation to the patriarchal state. It is interesting that the Christian virgin Agnes, who fiercely rejects Athena/Minerva and that model of virginity,

[13]See Marcel Detienne, *Dionysos Slain*, trans. Mireille Muellner and Leonard Muellner (Baltimore, 1979), pp. 33–34.
[14]Detienne, *Dionysos Slain*, pp. 25–26.

shares some characteristics of the mythic figures who inhabit the "terrain of the hunter." For in that terrain, chastity and refusal of marriage live side by side with sexual deviance of various kinds. In the story of Atalanta, for example, Atalanta's excessive devotion to Artemis and fear of marriage lead to Aphrodite's revenge. Fearing marriage, Atalanta flees to the woods and becomes a huntress in one version of the myth. In another version, she challenges her suitors to a footrace for which the winner will receive her in marriage as the prize, but the losers will die. With Aphrodite's help, Melanion (or Hippomenes in some variants) is able to distract her and win the race. Then Atalanta and her husband, made irrational by Aphrodite, make love in a temple like animals and are transformed into lions. Atalanta moves from total chastity to excessive and improper sexuality without occupying the middle ground of fruitful marriage.

The components of Prudentius' poem reflect this model of virginity, for Agnes, too, is a marginal figure who oscillates between sexual extremes. Her rejection of both men and the virginity exemplified by Minerva give her masculine characteristics, enabling her to take up arms (the thunderbolt), render her opponent impotent, and celebrate a triumph. In all of this she closely resembles the Amazons, a race of warrior women who live apart from men and reject domesticity. But, like Atalanta, who tries to shun marriage and ends up punished for sexual deviance, Agnes, through the brothel scene, is closely associated with sexual excess and is punished (or rewarded) by a death that renders her sexually neutral.

The origin of the story of the virgin in the brothel is unclear,[15] but Prudentius appears to be the first to associate it with Agnes. His younger contemporary Palladius includes a similar story in his *Lausiac History*, written in 419–420, but the

---

[15]There is a strikingly similar incident in Seneca the Elder's *Controversiae* 1.2, in which a virgin is kidnapped by pirates and forced to work in a brothel. She claims to have preserved her chastity; when a soldier tried to rape her, she killed him. When she was finally returned to her family, she sought to become a priestess.

nameless heroine of his tale is clearly not Agnes, for he describes her as being from Corinth. In his version of the story, a beautiful Corinthian girl who was contemplating taking a vow of virginity was denounced before the magistrates and charged with blaspheming the emperors and the gods. The magistrate in charge of the case had her put in a brothel, where she repelled her clients by telling them she had a dreadful sore in a hidden place that emitted an intolerable odor and that they should come back next week.[16] Finally, a young man came to the brothel, pretended to hire her services, gave her his clothes, and helped her escape, for which he was martyred by being thrown to the beasts in the arena.[17] Palladius tells of reading this story in an old book "under the name of Hippolytus" (*Hist. Laus.* 65.1)—presumably the name of the hero of the tale who, like the other characters named Hippolytus we have encountered, suffers a form of dismemberment when he is thrown to the wild beasts in the arena. It is unlikely that Palladius borrowed the story from Prudentius: more probably they had a common source.

It is surely not simply coincidence that this folk legend repeated by Palladius associates chastity, prostitution, reversal of sexual roles (the girl dressing as a man while he takes her place inside the brothel), and death by wild beasts with a young hero named Hippolytus. This constellation of motifs is so similar to those of the myth of Hippolytus and Phaedra that the only surprising aspect about the recycling of the story is that Prudentius did not include it in his poem about Saint Hippolytus.[18] The virgin-in-the-brothel tale corresponds quite pre-

[16]This detail clearly resembles the bad smell with which Venus punishes the Lemnian women and the odor of fasting women performing the Thesmophoria, an Athenian festival in honor of Demeter. For more about these, see Zeitlin, "Cultic Models of the Female," and Walter Burkert, "Jason, Hypsipyle, and New Fire at Lemnos," *CQ* 20 (1970):1–16.

[17]Palladius, *La Storia Lausiaca,* ed. G. M. J. Bartelink, trans. Marino Barchiesi (1978), chap. 65.

[18]It seems likely that Prudentius, in composing the Hippolytus poem, came across the tale we find in Palladius and chose to reserve it for the Agnes poem, in which he concentrates on the issue of sexuality.

cisely to the cluster of myths Detienne has analyzed, myths that define marriage by opposing it to abstinence and excess, and thus is appropriate to a poem whose subject is virginity. The difference, of course, is that the rejection of the societal values of marriage and procreation that Atalanta, Hippolytus, and Adonis represent has, in the Christian story, been valorized. A new moral has been added to an old fable.

Prudentius was writing at a time when the ancient paradigm of sexuality was just beginning to be redefined by the impact of the ascetic movement that began in Egypt in the fourth century. The new ideal of virginity did not enter into the mainstream of Late Roman thought without a struggle, a struggle we can see overtly expressed by the critics of Jerome's efforts to convert noble Roman ladies to the ascetic life.[19] For the majority of Christians in the fourth and early fifth centuries, sexuality was, in the words of Peter Brown, "treated as an unproblematic because, in the last analysis, a detachable component of human nature."[20] Marriage and the adherence to the biblical order to "Go forth and multiply" were judged to be good things, not evidences of the Fall, and for those who chose to lead the spiritual life, the common thing to do was what Paulinus of Nola and many others did—marry, reproduce, and then retire from the world, or live with one's spouse as sister and brother. As was the case in Athens in the fifth century B.C., sexuality was "securely harnessed to marriage and to childbirth" even while sexual continence was admired.[21]

As Brown has shown, the model of sexuality adopted by Western society was about to undergo a radical transition from the long-held "civic" view that sexuality was, essentially, a matter of reproduction, to the darker Augustinian view that sexuality was dislocated, indiscriminate, and barely able to be

[19]See J. N. D. Kelly's *Jerome: His Life, Writings, and Controversies* (London, 1975), pp. 107–113, for the controversy resulting in Jerome's departure from Rome, and Jerome's extraordinary letter *In Eustochium*.

[20] Brown, "Sexuality and Society in the Fifth Century A.D.: Augustine and Julian of Eclanum," in *Scritti in onore di Arnaldo Momigliano*, ed. E. Gabba (Como, 1983), p. 55.

[21]Ibid., p. 57.

restrained by the curbs of society.[22] In the older model, both
excessive abstinence and extramarital sex constitute a threat to
civic life, whereas in the newer model virginity is the highest
good and uncontrollable human urges are a threat to it. In the
Agnes poem, Prudentius seems to be applying the older paradigm to the newly defined virtue of virginity—hence, perhaps,
some of the tensions and seeming incongruities we perceive in
his portrayal of Agnes. For he links Agnes' virginity, almost by
reflex, with that other threat to stable marriage, prostitution: a
move no more surprising than Ovid's decision to place the
story of Atalanta, the huntress who tries to reject marriage,
inside the story of Adonis, the perfumed seducer unable to
survive in the terrain of the hunter.

Unlike Atalanta, of course, Agnes is triumphant: she is able
to maintain her chastity. But the sexual crisis in the text does
not end with the triumphant resolution of the brothel scene, as
it does in Palladius' more folkloric version of the story. For
Agnes herself displays an extreme and rather morbid eroticism in her final speech. Indeed this final speech is disturbing
enough to have evoked the dismay of Lavarenne, the editor of
the Budé edition of Prudentius, who says in his introduction to
the poem, "When she sees the executioner, Agnes delivers a
tirade of sixteen verses (69–84) shamefullly lacking in inno-
cence. . . . Once more Prudentius has chosen a beautiful subject, but has not been able to produce from it a poem anyone
could like."[23] More than just lacking in simplicity, Agnes'
speech makes it only too clear that she explicitly envisions her
death as a sexual act, and one she welcomes. Her executioner
appears in her fantasy as a lover, and her goal is to draw the
vim, the violence and strength, of the phallic sword into herself:

> exulto talis quod potius venit
> vesanus, atrox, turbidus armiger,

[22]Ibid., pp. 64–65.
[23]*Oeuvres,* ed. and trans. M. Laverenne (Paris, 1955), vol. 4, p. 195, my
translation.

> quam si veniret languidus ac tener
> mollisque ephebus tinctus aromate,
> qui me pudoris funere perderet.
> hic, hic amator, iam fateor, placet:
> ibo inruentis gressibus obviam,
> nec demorabor vota calentia:
> ferrum in papillas omne recepero
> pectusque ad imum vim gladii traham.
>
> *(Perist.* 14.69–79)

I rejoice to see such a frenzied, fierce, disturbed man of weapons, far more than I would if he came limp and soft, a delicate youth dripping perfume who would ruin me and kill my chastity. Now I confess it—this man is the lover who pleases me! When he forces himself on me, I will meet him halfway. I will not put off (his?) burning desire: I will take his whole sword into my breasts and draw the force of his blade deep into my heart.

Agnes views her death as a seduction that will allow her to appropriate the *vim gladii* (force of his blade) of her oppressor. Her erotic death by phallic sword thrust is strongly reminiscent of Phaedra's passionate wish that Hippolytus stab her, which would allow her death to be the consummation of her love for him at the same time that it would ensure her chastity. Hippolytus, appalled by the erotic overtones of her speech, flings away his sword and flees, denying her the death she craves, just as Agnes, in the end, does not receive the penetrating thrust of the executioner's sword, but is instead abruptly beheaded.[24]

[24]Phaedra's speech to Hippolytus, begging him to kill her:

> *Phaedra:* Hippolyte, nunc me compotem voti facis;
> sanas furentem. Maius hoc voto meo est,
> salvo ut pudore manibus immoriar tuis.
> *Hippolytus:* Abscede, vive ne quid exores, et hic
> contactus ensis deserat castum latus.
>
> *(Phaedra* 710–714)

Phaedra: Hippolytus, now you grant my prayer; now you heal my madness. This is even more than my prayer, that I might die by your hand, with my honor intact. *Hippolytus:* Go away! Live, rather than get your wish. And let this sword which has touched you leave my chaste side.

The death Agnes has in mind for herself reflects her self-image. The death by sword she desired is, in addition to its erotic aspects, the paradigm of "masculine" death, the "pure" death by the sword, as Nicole Loraux has pointed out.[25] Women's deaths, Loraux claims in her analysis of ways to kill women in Greek tragedy, are characterized by hanging, knots, and snares. To die by the sword or the dagger is to steal from men their death. Men die at their posts, like soldiers; women "escape" into death by leaping or hanging (metaphorically equivalent to leaping because the victim swings in the air). If we place Agnes' death in this scheme, we see that she attempts to usurp this masculine death by the sword, just as she has (briefly) appropriated the phallic thunderbolt.

Here the text seems to strain in two directions. On the one hand, Agnes achieves the triumph of the "masculine" death by the sword she craves. On the other hand, her death is not as she had envisioned. It is surely worth noting that the death by stabbing which she anticipates in such erotic detail proves not to be her fate. It is replaced, without any comment in the text, by death by decapitation. Agnes, in fact, suffers the fate of Medusa, unexpectedly losing her head in a symbolic castration. She becomes a female eunuch, forced to exchange the role of Zeus for that of Ganymede—for the unsexing, the loss of female sexuality achieved by her decapitation, is immediately reflected in the text. The grammatical subject changes instantly from the feminine Agnes to her masculine *spiritus,* and it is this masculine part of her that finally makes the transcendent leap to the stars. Like the nameless maiden in Palladius' story, who flees from the brothel dressed as a man, she can escape only in male guise.

We now see some of the reasons for Lavarenne's conclusion that this is not a poem anyone could like. Agnes is an extremely

---

See Petrucione, "Prudentius' Use of Martyrological Topoi," pp. 101–104, on the different versions of Agnes' death; Lavarenne briefly mentions the variants in his introduction to *Peristephanon* 14.

[25]*Tragic Ways of Killing a Woman,* trans. Anthony Forster (Cambridge, Mass., 1987).

unstable figure as she oscillates between victimized virgin and powerful, Medusa-like figure: between aggressive female sexuality and masculine attributes and language. Whatever Prudentius' intentions in writing this poem, in the end he produced a paradox. Agnes, a Christian heroine espousing the new Christian concept of virginity, has the same characteristic sexual ambivalence as Atalanta, who, in Ovid's tale, goes from being fiercely opposed to sex to being overly eager for sex, and ends up, essentially, desexed. Agnes, though she maintains her virginal status, follows a similar path, moving from declared virginity to the brothel and her seductive speech to the executioner, to her death and transformation into a grammatically masculine, incorporeal spirit, safely surrounded by angels as she heads toward the interior of her Father's house.

Prudentius Crowned

As we have seen, the alternation between two models of female sexuality—the aggressive, seductive, wolfish sexuality of Agnes as *lupa* and the repressive abstinence of virginity—dominates the poem's action. This duality that defines Agnes is also an essential aspect of the plant that shares her name— the *agnus castus* tree. This plant was used to ensure ritual sexual abstinence in women at religious festivals and to promote lactation and fertility. Furthermore, the tree was also known in Greek as the *lugos,* almost the equivalent of *lukos,* "wolf." We have already observed Prudentius' fascination with wordplays: in this cluster of words, he has what he needs to determine the structure of the poem. Agnes, whose name bears so many possible meanings, is at once victim (sacrificial lamb) and drug (*agnus castus*): truly a *pharmakon,* in both its senses, as sacrificial scapegoat and as seductively dangerous but potentially healing drug.

The *agnus castus* plant was used at the Thesmophoria, an Athenian festival in honor of Demeter that was held each year and attended by the wives of Athenian citizens. These women had to abstain from sex for three days; to aid them in maintaining this ritual period of chastity, they made themselves mats woven from the branches of the *agnus castus* tree. As Froma Zeitlin observes:

> Inherent in this harnessing of the powers of female fecundity which necessitates an active, even violent, role for women, is the anxiety which surrounds the giving of power to women, power that is as close to parthenogenesis as possible. Male symbolism is not absent in the rite, but is merely an adjunct, reduced to instrumental terms, objects which the women handle and use to enhance their own dominant role in procreation. That role is paradoxically more clearly defined by the cultic chastity, which seems to separate sexuality and fertility even as it separates male and female spaces. The *agnus castus* plant upon which the women sat is emblematic of this division, for while it was thought to possess antaphrodisiac qualities, it was also believed to stimulate fertility in women by encouraging menstruation and lactation. But that same separation is potentially too great . . . [recalling] the continuing Greek fantasy, the Amazon complex, one might say, which envisions a society, an alternate structure composed only of women and innately hostile to men, whom they want to dominate, use, and rule.[26]

The *agnus castus* plant has the power, in the sphere of female fertility, both to bind women in unnatural abstinence and to stimulate their fertility by releasing the flow of menstrual blood and milk. It seems likely that the mat-weaving at the Athenian festival was meant to ensure that it was the plant's binding power, not its releasing power, that was invoked.

Thus the *agnus castus* has the same sexual ambivalence as the virginal Agnes—though the plant alternates between socially approved, limited, ritual abstinence and fertility, thus circumscribing sexuality within marriage, while Agnes, alternating between permanent abstinence and prostitution, defines sexuality outside of marriage. The association of the tree with chastity was know in the Christian period—the bishop Meth-

[26]Zeitlin, "Cultic Models of the Female," p. 146.

odius, in his heavily Platonic *Symposium* (*Banquet*), has his speakers (all virgins) assemble in an idyllic rural spot under the branches of an *agnus castus* tree, where they proceed to hold a dialogue on the virtues of virginity.[27]

But the significance of the *agnus castus* is not limited to the sphere of female sexuality. We have the fragmentary evidence of another myth involving the tree, which Vernant and Detienne present in their discussion of the battle of wits between Prometheus and Zeus. According to a fragment of the *Prometheus Unbound,* it is in honor of Prometheus that the custom of wearing crowns or garlands was established. For Prometheus, when released from his chains, received a crown *antipoina tou ekeinou desmou,* "in exchange for his bonds"—a crown made from the twigs of the *lugos,* "willow tree." Athenaeus explains, in his commentary, that the crown is the penance assigned by Zeus in exchange for his freedom. Vernant and Detienne link the woven willow crown with the cunning binding power of *metis* (craft or cunning intelligence), commenting:

> On the basis of this text where the crown of willow is, to be sure, reminiscent of his earlier chains but where at the same time the bonds . . . are transformed into a crown of victory, it is not easy to see which of the two . . . has really won a definitive victory over his opponent in this contest of binding and unbinding which *metis* presides over.[28]

When we combine this fragmentary myth with the evidence from the ritual of the Thesmophoria, it seems likely that the power of the chaste tree lies not only in its specifically sexual function, but in its command over the power, associated with *metis,* of binding and releasing.

The correspondence between Prudentius' young martyr Agnes and the *agnus castus* tree is revealed in the tight network of overlapping meanings among the group *agnus*/*hagnos*/

[27]Methodius *Symp.,* preface, sect. 8; the symbolism of the *agnus castus* is further discussed in the tenth conversation, sect. 265.
[28]Vernant and Detienne, *Cunning Intelligence,* pp. 84–85.

Agnes and *lugos/lukos/lupa.* Agnes, the virgin who finds herself in a brothel, the martyr who prefers death to sex but who welcomes her executioner with an overwhelmingly erotic speech, embodies the paradoxical powers of the plant. The persistent conflict between the constricting language of the text, which repeatedly confines and encloses Agnes, and her ostensible liberation from bondage through death is epitomized in the *duplex corona* she receives after death. Like the crown of willow Prometheus receives in exchange for his chains, it is a symbol at once of bondage and of freedom.

But the crown is something more. In the scheme of the *Peristephanon* as a whole, the crown is a frequent symbol of poetry as well as of martyrdom; in particular, it represents the poet's own verse. It is a symbol of his *metis,* his practical ability to weave words together into song.[29] The imagery of bondage which permeates the *Peristephanon,* a book abounding in knots, chains, ropes, snares, and various forms of constraint and deceit, is balanced by the persistent image of binding and weaving as a metaphor for creation, just as the frequent images of dissolution, amputation, and dismemberment are offset by more positive images of liberation and freedom. Prudentius' task as a poet is to maintain a delicate balance between the forces of binding and unbinding, but as he weaves together the fabric of his own creation, he finds himself perilously close to usurping the function of God, whose creative power Prudentius consistently represents as a form of binding or weaving. Prudentius, even as he exercises the poet's binding art, runs the risk of becoming a second Prometheus, Zeus' rival for the creative, binding force of *metis.* I believe Prudentius had this comparison in mind, for he closes the *Peristephanon* with this final prayer to Agnes:

[29]See, for example, *Perist.* 3.206–210, in which Prudentius offers garlands of (wilted) verses to Eulalia, the other virgin celebrated in the *Peristephanon:* "ista comantibus e foliis / munera, virgo puerque, date! / Ast ego serta choro in medio / texta feram pede dactylico, / vilia, marcida, festa tamen" (Girl and boy, give her these gifts from flowing leaves. But from the middle of the chorus I will bring garlands woven in dactylics—cheap and withered, but festive nonetheless).

purgabor oris propitiabilis
fulgore, nostrum si iecur inpleas.
nil non pudicum est quod pia visere
dignaris almo vel pede tangere.

(Perist. 14.130–133)

I shall be cleansed by the flashing fire of your kind face, if you fill up my heart/liver. Loyal girl, nothing is unchaste that you deign to touch with your gracious foot.

Metaphorically restoring the power of Zeus' thunderbolt to Agnes (her face will cleanse him with its fire), Prudentius asks her, rather oddly, to fill up his liver: *si iecur inpleas.* The liver, of course, was traditionally the seat of emotion and particularly of passion, and so its presence here reinforces the erotic overtones of the hymn to Agnes. But it may play another role here as well. Just as Prudentius alerts his readers to the presence of an anagram at the end of the *Hamartigenia* by a combination of odd syntax and a pun on his own name (see Chapter 2), so here he ends this poem, ostensibly in praise of virginity, on an incongruous note, by asking rather illogically for the renewal of his *iecur,* the most passionate and least rational part of himself. And, once again, the riddle posed by the slightly incongruous ending of the poem signals the identity and the presence of the poet.

In this passage it is as if Prudentius, adopting the role of Prometheus (whose punishment included the daily agony of having his liver devoured by Zeus' eagle), has armed his own creation in the panoply of Zeus and now looks to her for release. He even appeals to Agnes' *pietas,* loyalty she surely owes to him, her creator. Prudentius, a poet clearly fascinated by names and etymologies and fond of bilingual Greek and Latin puns, would hardly have overlooked the fact that his own name, *Prudentius* (foresight), is a good Latin translation of the name of the Titan *Prometheus* (forethought). Thus ambivalent Agnes, whose trials complete the garland of the *Peristephanon,* becomes the equivalent of Prometheus' willow crown: the symbol of Prudentius' mastery of the creative force of poetic binding as well as of the chains of the flesh from which he longs to escape.

Conclusion

The *Peristephanon* is a curious literary document, but one that rewards close study. I have chosen to focus on aspects of the poem which have not yet been treated by other scholars, particularly on Prudentius' reliance on the structural framework of classical myth in his narratives and on certain features of his poetic technique, including his use of wordplay. This is not the usual or, perhaps, the obvious way to approach Prudentius, but it is, I think, a useful one, especially because it serves as a counterweight to much of the work on Prudentius so far—work that is thorough and often quite sensitive, but that has sometimes seemed patronizing or based on outmoded assumptions about Latin poetry and about the fourth and fifth centuries.

A conclusive study of Prudentius remains to be written. This book is concerned mostly with only one of Prudentius' poetic books and does not pretend to be exhaustive. Despite this focus, I hope I have suggested new ways to approach not only Prudentius, but also other Late Antique poets, who offer students of classical Latin poetry a refreshing combination of the familiar and the radically new.

We find this combination in the *Peristephanon,* a work in which Prudentius celebrates and also subjects to an almost cold analytical scrutiny the growing cult of the martyrs. He was clearly fascinated, even moved, by the stories of martyrdom he relates, but there is little doubt that he approached his material with a critical eye and shaped his narratives to suit his own purposes, which were not exclusively devotional and celebratory. Nowhere in the *Peristephanon* do we sense the same sort of close emotional bond between Prudentius and his subjects that Paulinus of Nola felt for Felix, or Sulpicius Severus for Saint Martin of Tours. Prudentius' martyrs are literary composites, almost as abstract as the allegorical characters who fight their way through the *Psychomachia*. They are not realistic characters, nor are they, except in name, much like the "very special dead" whose protection comforted so many Late Antique men and women.[30] The hymns that celebrate them explore serious issues, often in unexpected ways, and the way the character of a martyr in any given poem is determined has less to do with what Prudentius found in the hagiographic tradition than with whatever intellectual construct he happens to be exploring.

Hippolytus, for example, a schismatic priest, suffers the same death as Claudian's Rufinus and Prudentius' own Discordia after a conversion that brings him back to orthodoxy. But the poem as Prudentius constructed it is more than a celebration of the return of a heretic to the fold. Prudentius exploits the saint's name, which is identical to that of the mythical Hippolytus, by hinting at underlying similarities between Christian history and pagan mythology. As if to ensure his reader's awareness of this doubling of identities, he describes at length a tomb painting that purports to illustrate the death of Saint Hippolytus, though in fact it is a painting of a standard pagan type depicting the death of the mythical Hippolytus. Because Prudentius elsewhere describes what appears to be an identical painting on the wall of a temple to Diana Trivia, it seems he is either inventing the Christian catacomb painting or that he is at least aware of its ambiguity. Rather than simply repeating the tale of the martyrdom of Saint Hippolytus, Prudentius uses the coincidence of the names and the ambiguity of the painting to transform his hymn into a meditation on the relationship between Christian and pagan myth.

In *Peristephanon* 13 we find another case of grafting. This time Prudentius has conflated the story of the martyrdom of the sober Cyprian of Carthage with the romantic adventures of the improbably seductive Cyprian of Antioch; on top of this he has added what appears to be his own version of the martyrdom of the Candida Massa. As often happens in Pruden-

[30]Peter Brown, *The Cult of the Saints: Its Rise and Function in Latin Christianity* (Chicago, 1981), p. 70.

tius' verse, the incongruities and inconsistencies call attention to the underlying issues of the poem. Cyprian's abrupt transformation from a beautiful, seductive, but sterile youth into an old man whose passionate rhetoric inspires the Candida Massa to leap to their death suggests a connection between the young Cyprian's magical rhetoric of seduction and the older Cyprian's erotic rhetoric of martyrdom. This combination of seduction, sterility, and death looks odd from a Christian standpoint, but Cyprian's name marks him as a man of Venus, and in the components of his character that Prudentius stresses, we can see a marked resemblance to Adonis, another protegé of the Cyprian goddess.

Peristephanon 13 is an Ovidian poem. Not only does Cyprian behave like one of Ovid's lovely youths and undergo a sudden metamorphosis, but the Candida Massa undergo a remarkable transformation as well in a ludicrous scene that reverses Ovid's account of the creation of the world in *Metamorphoses* 1. Prudentius has wandered far from the martyrdom of Cyprian of Carthage, which was well attested and with which his audience must have been familiar. As I have suggested, one way to interpret this portrayal of Cyprian and his followers, which is not entirely positive, is to assume that it was influenced by accounts of the extremist element in the Donatist church, who actively sought martyrdom in a way contemporary orthodox Christians dismissed as suicidal, and who looked on Cyprian as their patron saint.

The hymn to Agnes which closes the *Peristephanon* is, in some ways, Prudentius' tour de force. Undoubtedly inspired by the potential for wordplay, Prudentius added to the story of Agnes' martyrdom the tale of a virgin's trial by brothel, making it the focal point of the poem, which is a study of virginity. It is an intriguing poem partly because Prudentius seems, in a sense, to be translating the relatively new concept of perpetual virginity back into the classical idiom. Agnes, the modest martyr, oscillates wildly between sexual extremes, just as the language of the poem oscillates between confinement and release, as if Prudentius were unable to break free of the classical paradigm in which abstinence stands next to sexual excess and deviance as a threat to fruitful marriage.

Like the characters of Hippolytus and Cyprian, Agnes' character is determined to some extent by the meaning of her name and by the series of puns it generates on wolves, sheep, prostitutes, and the chaste tree. It seems that for Prudentius language is supercharged with meaning. Words, for him, are entities—it is not simply coincidence that he is the inventor of personification allegory. His verse operates by a kind of semantic determinism: his characters seem fated to live up to the full potential of their names.

The poet does not exclude himself from this process. He casts himself as a Promethean figure, with all that the comparison implies. Prometheus is the archetypal creative artist in classical mythology. He makes men from clay and brings them to life, then tricks Zeus and steals the divine fire to give to the men he created. For this he is horribly punished, chained to a rock with his liver devoured each day by Zeus' eagle and renewed each night. But his punishment does not last forever. Prometheus' *metis,* the binding power that he, more than any other figure in Greek myth, commands, becomes necessary to Zeus, who after an eternity sends his son Heracles to free Prometheus from his chains. And, as we have seen, in some versions of the myth Prometheus exchanges his bonds for the ambiguous crown woven from the twigs of the *agnus castus* tree.

Prudentius also possesses *metis.* He, too, is chained; he speaks frequently of the chains of the flesh and hopes for ultimate freedom, a freedom he hopes to achieve through the liberating power of his poetry. In the *Peristephanon,* the garland of hymns which is the ultimate example of his poetic prowess, he has woven the crown he hopes will replace and commemorate his bonds, as Prometheus' willow crown finally replaced and commemorated his chains.

Selected Bibliography

This bibliography contains only works cited in the text and is not comprehensive.

Ahl, Frederick M. "The Art of Safe Criticism in Greece and Rome." *AJPh* 105 (1984):174–208.
———. *Lucan: An Introduction.* Ithaca, N.Y.: Cornell University Press, 1976.
———. *Metaformations: Soundplay and Wordplay in Ovid and Other Classical Poets.* Ithaca, N.Y.: Cornell University Press, 1985.
———. "The Rider and the Horse: Politics and Power in Roman Poetry from Horace to Statius." *ANRW* 2, no. 1 (1984):40–110.
Aristotle. *Metaphysics.* Edited and translated by Hugh Tredennick. New York: G. P. Putnam's Sons, Loeb Classical Library, 1933.
———. *Nichomachean Ethics.* Edited and translated by H. Rackham. New York: G. P. Putnam's Sons, Loeb Classical Library, 1926.
Ausonius. *Opuscula.* Edited by Sextus Prete. Leipzig: Teubner, 1978.
———. *Works.* Edited and translated by H. G. Evelyn White. New York: G. P. Putnam's Sons, Loeb Classical Library, 1919.
Bertonière, Gabriel. *The Cult Center of the Martyr Hippolytus on the Via Tiburtina.* Oxford: British Academy in Rome, International Series no. 260, 1985.
Brisson, Jean-Paul. *Autonomisme et Christianisme dans l'Afrique romaine de Septime Sévère à l'invasion vandale.* Paris: de Boccard, 1958.
Brown, Peter Robert Lamont. *Augustine of Hippo.* Berkeley: University of California Press, 1967.
———. *The Cult of the Saints: Its Rise and Function in Latin Christianity.* Chicago: University of Chicago Press, 1981.

——. *The Making of Late Antiquity.* Cambridge: Harvard University Press, 1978.

——. "Sexuality and Society in the Fifth Century A.D.: Augustine and Julian of Eclanum." In *Scritti in onore di Arnaldo Momigliano,* edited by E. Gabba, pp. 49–70. Como: Edizioni New Press, 1983.

——. *Society and the Holy in Late Antiquity.* Berkeley: University of California Press, 1982.

——. *The World of Late Antiquity:* A.D. *150–750.* London: Thames & Hudson, 1971.

Brozek, M. "De librorum Prudentii inscriptionibus graecis." *Eos* 71 (1983):191–197.

Burkert, Walter. "Jason, Hypsipyle, and New Fire at Lemnos." *CQ* 20 (1970):1–16.

Cameron, Alan. *Claudian: Poetry and Propaganda at the Court of Honorius.* Oxford: Clarendon Press, 1970.

Chadwick, Henry. *Priscillian of Avila: The Occult and the Charismatic in the Early Church.* New York: Oxford University Press, 1976.

Charlet, J. L. "L'influence d'Ausone sur la poésie de Prudence." Diss., Sorbonne, 1972.

Cicero. *De Natura Deorum.* Edited by Wilhelm Ax. Leipzig: Teubner, 1961.

Claudian. *Claudii Claudiani Carmina.* Edited by John Barrie Hall. Leipzig: Teubner, 1985.

——. *In Rufinum.* Edited by Harry Levy. New York, 1935.

Costanza, Salvatore. "Rapporti letterari tra Paolino e Prudenzio." In *Atti del convegno 31 cinquantenario della morte di S. Paolino de Nola (431–1981),* Nola, March 20–21, 1982. Rome: Herder, 1983.

Delehaye, Hippolyte. "Cyprien d'Antioche et Cyprien de Carthage." *Analecta Bollandiana* 39 (1921):314–322.

——. "Recherches sur le legendier romain." *Analecta Bollandiana* 51 (1933):34–98.

Detienne, Marcel. *Dionysos Slain.* Translated by Mireille Muellner and Leonard Muellner. Baltimore: Johns Hopkins University Press, 1979. Originally published as *Dionysos mis à mort* (Paris: Gallimard, 1977).

——. *The Gardens of Adonis: Spices in Greek Mythology.* Translated by Janet Lloyd. Sussex: Humanities Press, 1977. Originally published as *Les Jardins d'Adonis: La mythologie des aromates en Grèce* (Paris: Bibliothèque des Histoires, 1972).

Selected Bibliography

Detienne, Marcel, and Jean-Pierre Vernant. *Cunning Intelligence in Greek Culture and Society.* Translated by Janet Lloyd. Brighton: Harvester Press, 1978. Originally published as *Les Ruses de l'intelligence: La Métis des Grecs* (Paris: Flammarion, 1974).

Diodorus Siculus. *Bibliothèque Historique.* Edited and translated by Michel Casevitz. Paris: Les Belles Lettres, 1972.

Dumézil, Georges. *Archaic Roman Religion.* Translated by Philip Krapp. Chicago: University of Chicago Press, 1970. Originally published as *La Religion romaine archaïque* (Paris: Payot, 1966).

Evenepoel, W. "La présence d'Ovide dans l'oeuvre de Prudence." *Caesarodunum* 17 bis (1982):165–176.

Ferrua, Antonio. *Le pitture della Nuova Catacomba di Via Latina.* Vatican City: Pontificio Istituto di Archeologia Cristiana, Monumenta di Antichità Cristiana Series 2, 1960.

Fevrier, P-A., and R. Guéry. "Les Rites funéraires de la Nécropole de Sétif." *Antiquités Africaines* 15 (1980):91–124.

Fitzgerald, William. "Aeneas, Daedalus and the Labyrinth." *Arethusa* 17 (1984):51–65.

Fontaine, Jacques. *Études sur la poésie latine tardive d'Ausone à Prudence.* Paris: Les Belles Lettres, 1980.

———. *Naissance de la poésie latine dans l'occident chrétien: Esquisse d'une histoire de la poésie chrétienne du IIIe au VIe siècle.* Paris: Études Augustiniennes, 1981.

Franchi, Pietro de'Cavalieri. "S. Agnese nella tradizione e nella leggenda." *ST* 221 (1962):292–381.

Frend, W. H. C. "The *cellae* of the African Circumcellions." *JTS* n.s. 3 (1952):87–89.

———. *The Donatist Church: A Movement of Protest in Roman North Africa.* Oxford: Clarendon Press, 1952.

———. *Religion Popular and Unpopular in the Early Christian Centuries.* London: Variorum Reprints, 1976.

———. *The Rise of Christianity.* London: Darton, Longman and Todd, 1984.

Garthwaite, John. "Appendix: Statius' *Silvae* 3.4: On the Fate of Earinus." *ANRW* 2, no. 1 (1984):111–124.

Gnilka, Christian. *Studien zur "Psychomachie" des Prudentius.* Wiesbaden: Otto Harrassowitz, 1963.

Grimal, Pierre. *La guerre civile de Petrone dans ses rapports avec la Pharsale.* Paris: Les Belles Lettres, 1977.

Selected Bibliography

Guarducci, Margherita. "La statua di 'Sant' Ippolito.'" In *Ricerche su Ippolito*, pp. 17–30. Studia Ephemeridis Augustinianum 13. Rome: Institutum Patristicum Augustinianum, 1977.

Harries, Jill. "Prudentius and Theodosius." *Latomus* 43 (1984):69–84.

Haworth, Kenneth R. *Deified Virtues, Demonic Vices, and Descriptive Allegory in Prudentius' "Psychomachia."* Amsterdam: Adolf M. Hakkert, 1980.

Henderson, W. J. "Violence in Prudentius' Peristephanon." *Akroterion* 28 (1983):84–92.

Herzog, Reinhart. *Die allegorische Dichtkunst des Prudentius. Zetemata* vol. 42. Munich: Beck, 1966.

Honoré, Tony. "*Scriptor Historiae Augustae.*" *JRS* 77 (1987):156–176.

Horace. *Opera.* Edited by David R. Shackleton Bailey. Stuttgart: Teubner, 1983.

Kelly, J. N. D. *Jerome: His Life, Writings, and Controversies.* London: Duckworth, 1975.

Künzle, Paul. "Bemerkungen zum Lob auf Sankt Peter und Sankt Paul von Prudentius (*Perist.* 12)." *Rivista di Storia della Chiesa in Italia* 11 (1957):309–370.

Lamberton, Robert. *Homer the Theologian: Neoplatonist Allegorical Reading and the Growth of the Epic Tradition.* Berkeley: University of California Press, 1986.

Lana, Italo. *Due capitoli prudenziani: La biografia, la cronologia delle opere, la poetica.* Verbum Seniorum, collana di testi e studi patristici, n.s. 2. Rome: Editrice Studium, 1962.

Lapidge, Michael. "A Stoic Metaphor in Late Latin Poetry: The Binding of the Cosmos." *Latomus* 39 (1980):817–837.

Leglay, Marcel. *Saturne africain: Histoire.* Paris: de Boccard, 1966.

Lepelley, Claude. "*Iuvenes* et Circoncellions: Les derniers sacrifices humaines de l'Afrique antique." *Antiquités Africaines* 15 (1980): 261–272.

Levitan, William. "Dancing at the End of the Rope: Optatian and the Field of Roman Verse." *TAPhA* 115 (1985):245–269.

——. "Plexed Artistry: Three Aratean Acrostics." *Glyph* 5 (1976):55–68.

Lewis, C. S. *The Allegory of Love.* Rev. ed. Oxford: Clarendon Press, 1973.

Loi, Vicenzo. "La problematica storio-letteraria su Ippolito di Roma."

Selected Bibliography

In *Ricerche su Ippolito,* pp. 9–16. Studia Ephemeridis Augustinianum 13. Rome: Institutum Patristicum Augustinianum, 1977.

Loraux, Nicole. *Tragic Ways of Killing a Woman.* Translated by Anthony Forster. Cambridge: Harvard University Press, 1987. Originally published as *Façons tragiques de tuer une femme* (Paris: Hachette, 1985).

Lucan. *Belli Civilis Libri Decem.* Edited by A. E. Housman. Oxford: Blackwell, 1927.

Lucretius. *T. Lucreti Cari De Rerum Natura Libri Sex.* Edited by Joseph Martin. Leipzig: Teubner, 1969.

Mahoney, Albertus. "Vergil in the Works of Prudentius." Diss., Catholic University of America, Washington, D.C., 1934.

Markus, R. A. *From Augustine to Gregory the Great.* London: Variorum Reprints, 1983.

Matthews, John. "Gallic Supporters of Theodosius." *Latomus* 30 (1971):1073–1099.

———. "The Historical Setting of the *Carmen contra paganos* (Cod. Par. Lat. 8084)." *Historia* 20 (1970):464–479.

———. *Western Aristocracies and the Imperial Court: A.D. 364–425.* Oxford: Clarendon Press, 1975.

Methodius. *Le Banquet.* Edited by Herbert Musurillo. Translation and Notes by Victor-Henry Debidour. Paris: Éditions du Cerf, 1963.

Musurillo, Herbert, ed. *The Acts of the Christian Martyrs.* Oxford: Clarendon Press, 1972.

Nicephorus Callistus. *Ecclesiastica Historia. Patrologia cursus completus: Series Graeca,* vol. 145. Edited by J. P. Migne. Paris: J. P. Migne, 1857–1903.

Nugent, S. Georgia. *Allegory and Poetics: The Structure and Imagery of Prudentius' "Psychomachia."* Studien zur klassischen Philologie 14. Frankfurt: Lang, 1985.

———. "Vice and Virtue in Allegory: Reading Prudentius' *Psychomachia.*" Diss., Cornell University, 1980.

Onians, John. *Art and Thought in the Hellenistic Age: The Greek World View, 350–50 B.C.* London: Thames & Hudson, 1979.

Opelt, Ilona. "Der Christenverfolger bei Prudentius." *Philologus* 111 (1967):242–257.

Optatian. *Publilii Optatiani Porfyrii Carmina,* 2 vols. Edited by Giovanni Polara. Turin: Paravia, 1973.

Ovid. *Metamorphoses.* Edited by W. S. Anderson. Leipzig: Teubner, 1977.

———. *Tristia.* Edited by Georg Luck. Heidelberg: Winter, 1967.

Palladius. *La Storia Lausiaca.* Edited by G. J. M. Bartelink. Introduction by Christine Mohrmann, translation by Marino Barchiesi. Verona: Mondadori, 1978.

Paulinus of Nola. *Sancti Pontii Meropi Paulini Nolani Carmina.* Edited by Guilelmus de Hartel. CSEL vol. 30. Leipzig: Freytag, 1894.

Pepin, Jean. "La theologie tripartite de Varron." *REA* 2 (1956):265–294.

Petronius. *The "Bellum Civile" of Petronius.* Translated by Florence T. Baldwin. New York: Columbia University Press, 1941.

Petrucione, John Francis. "Prudentius' Use of Martyrological Topoi in *Peristephanon.*" Diss., University of Michigan, 1985.

Pharr, Clyde, ed. *The Theodosian Code and Novels and the Sirmian Constitutions.* Princeton, N.J.: Princeton University Press, 1952.

Philostratus the Elder. *Philostratus "Imagines," Callistus "Descriptions."* Translated by Arthur Fairbanks. New York: G. P. Putnam's Sons, Loeb Classical Library, 1931.

Proba. *The Golden Bough, the Oaken Cross: The Vergilian Cento of Faltonia Betitia Proba.* Edition, translation, and commentary by Elizabeth A. Clark and Diane Hatch. Chico, Calif.: Scholars' Press, 1981.

Prudentius. *Aurelii Prudentii Clementis Carmina.* Edited by Maurice Cunningham. Corpus Christianorum Series Latina, vol. 126. Turnholt: Brepols, 1966.

———. *Hamartigenia.* Edited with translation and commentary by Roberto Palla. Pisa: Giardini Editori e Stampatori, 1981.

———. *Prudence: Oeuvres.* Edited and translated by Maurice Lavarenne. 4 vols. 2d ed. Paris: Les Belles Lettres, 1955.

———. *Prudentius.* Edited and translated by H. J. Thomson. 2 vols. Cambridge: Harvard University Press, Loeb Classical Library, 1962.

———. *Psychomachia: testo con introduzione e traduzione.* Edited by Emmanuele Rapisarda. Catania: Centro di Studi sull' Antico Cristianesimo, 1962.

Putnam, Michael. "Daedalus, Virgil, and the End of Art." *AJPh* 108 (1987):173–198.

Roberts, Michael. "The *Mosella* of Ausonius: An Interpretation." *TAPhA* 114 (1984):343–353.

——. "Paulinus' Poem 11, Virgil's First Eclogue, and the Limits of *Amicitia.*" *TAPhA* 115 (1985):271–282.

Rousselle, Aline. *Porneia: On Desire and the Body in Antiquity.* Translated by Felicia Pheasant. Oxford: Blackwell, 1988. Originally published as *Porneia* (Paris: Presses Universitaires de France, 1983).

——. "Quelques aspects de l'affaire Priscillianiste." *REA* 83 (1981): 85–96.

Sabattini, P. Tino Alberto. "S. Cipriano nella tradizione agiografica." *Rivista di Studi Classici* 21 (1973):181–204.

——. "Storia e leggenda nei *Peristephanon* di Prudenzio." *Rivista di Studi Classici* 20 (1973):187–221.

Salomonson, J. W. *Voluptatem spectandi non perdat sed mutet: Observations sur l'iconographie du martyre en Afrique romaine.* Amsterdam: North Holland, 1979.

Segal, Charles. "Senecan Baroque: The Death of Hippolytus in Seneca, Ovid and Euripides." *TAPhA* 114 (1984):311–336.

Seneca. *Tragoediae.* Edited by Otto Zwierlein. Oxford: Clarendon Press, 1986.

Seneca the Elder. *Annaei Senecae Oratorum et Rhetorum Sententiae, Divisiones, Colores.* Edited by Adolphus Kiessling. Leipzig: Teubner, 1872.

Shaw, B. D. "Bandits in the Roman Empire." *Past and Present* 105 (1984):3–52.

Silius Italicus. *Punica.* Edited and translated by J. D. Duff. 2 vols. Cambridge: Harvard University Press, 1976.

Smith, Macklin. *Prudentius' "Psychomachia:" A Reexamination.* Princeton, N.J.: Princeton University Press, 1976.

Snyder, Jane. *Puns and Poetry in Lucretius' "De Rerum Natura."* Amsterdam: B. Gruner, 1980.

Spence, Sarah. *Rhetorics of Reason and Desire: Vergil, Augustine, and the Troubadours.* Ithaca, N.Y.: Cornell University Press, 1988.

Springer, A. R. "Prudentius, Pilgrim and Poet: The Catacombs and Their Paintings as Inspiration for the *Liber Cathemerinon.*" Diss., University of Wisconsin at Madison, 1984.

Statius. *Silvae.* Edited by Aldo Marastoni. Leipzig: Teubner, 1970.

——. *Thebais.* Edited by Alfredus Klotz. Leipzig: Teubner, 1973.

Stevenson, James. *The Catacombs: Rediscovered Monuments of Early Christian Art.* London: Thames & Hudson, 1978.

Suetonius. *C. Suetoni Tranquili Quae Supersunt Omnia.* Edited by C. L. Roth. Leipzig: Teubner, 1893.

Teixidor, Javier. *The Pagan God: Popular Religion in the Greco-Roman Near East*. Princeton, N.J.: Princeton University Press, 1977.

Tertullian. *Apologia, De Spectaculis, Minucius Felix*. Edited and translated by T. R. Glover, Gerald Randall, and W. C. A. Kerr. New York: G. P. Putnam's Sons, Loeb Classical Library, 1931.

Testini, Pasquali. "Di alcune testimonianze relative a Ippolito." In *Ricerche su Ippolito*, pp. 45–63. Studia Ephemeridis Augustinianum 13. Rome: Institutum Patristicum Augustinianum, 1977.

——. "S. Ippolito all' isola sacra." *Rendiconti della Pontificia Accademia Romana d'Archeologia* 51 (1978):23–46.

Thraede, Klaus. *Studien zu Sprache und Stil des Prudentius*. Hypomnemata 13. Gottingen: Vandenhoeck & Ruprecht, 1965.

Thury, Eva M. "Lucretius' Poem as a *Simulacrum* of the Rerum Natura." *AJPh* 108 (1987):270–294.

Trapé, Agostino. "Augustinus et Varro." In *Atti del Congresso Internazionale di Studi Varroniani*, vol. 2, pp. 553–563. Rieti: Centro di studi Varroniani, 1976.

Vergil. *Aeneid*. Edited with commentary by R. D. Williams. 2 vols. London: Macmillan, 1972.

Witke, Charles. *Numen Litterarum: The Old and the New in Latin Poetry from Constantine to Gregory the Great*. Leiden: Brill, 1971.

Zahn, T. *Cyprian von Antiochen und die deutsche Faustsage*. Erlagen, 1882.

Zeitlin, Froma. "Cultic Models of the Female: Rites of Dionysos and Demeter." *Arethusa* 15 (1982):140–155.

Index of Passages Quoted

General Index

Library of Congress Cataloging-in-Publication Data

Malamud, Martha A., 1957–
  A poetics of transformation.

  (Cornell studies in classical philology; v. 49)
  Bibliography: p.
  Includes index.
  1. Prudentius, b. 348—Criticism and interpretation.
2. Christian poetry, Latin—History and criticism.
3. Mythology, Classical, in literature. I. Title.
II. Series.
PA6648.P7M34 1989   871'.01   88–43290
ISBN 0–8014–2249–3 (alk. paper)